Journey to Lean

Journey to Lean
Making Operational Change Stick

John Drew,

Blair McCallum

and

Stefan Roggenhofer

Published by
PALGRAVE MACMILLAN
Houndmills, Basingstoke, Hampshire RG21 6XS and
175 Fifth Avenue, New York, N. Y. 10010
Companies and representatives throughout the world

PALGRAVE MACMILLAN is the global academic imprint of the Palgrave Macmillan division of St. Martin's Press, LLC and of Palgrave Macmillan Ltd. Macmillan® is a registered trademark in the United States, United Kingdom and other countries. Palgrave is a registered trademark in the European Union and other countries.

ISBN 1–4039–1307–2

This book is printed on paper suitable for recycling and made from fully managed and sustained forest sources.

A catalogue record for this book is available from the British Library.

Library of Congress Catalog Card Number: 2004041589

11 10   9   8   7
10 09 08 07 06 05

Printed and bound in Great Britain by
Creative Print and Design (Wales), Ebbw Vale

This book is dedicated to our clients and colleagues who have made the journey to lean with us

CONTENTS

Contents

LIST OF FIGURES

Acknowledgements

This book has truly been a team effort. In particular, the authors would like to thank the following people for their important contributions:

Our families for their support and forbearance.
Many colleagues who read early drafts and provided valuable feedback.
Annie Stogdale for helping us with the early stages of the book.
Jill Willder for her rigour and attention to detail in copy-editing.
Fred Chevalier for drawing the cartoons.
Pom Somkabcharti and Martin Liu at Cyan Communications.

ABOUT THIS BOOK

These days, it seems that most industrial enterprises and many service companies claim to apply lean thinking in their operations. Many of them do indeed apply lean tools, but few have managed to reap the benefits that Toyota and others have achieved. This is odd, because Toyota welcomes executives from other companies who want to learn about the famous Toyota Production System. Thousands of visitors have toured its plants, yet it isn't afraid of giving away competitive advantage. The reason is that very few visitors understand the full story behind what they see, and even fewer can begin to emulate Toyota's approach in their own operations.

Toyota can be so confident because it knows that lean goes way beyond the application of lean tools. Its system has taken 50 years to develop, and has been shaped by historical constraints. After the Second World War, stringent labour regulations made it much harder for Japanese employers to lay people off. Toyota found a way to turn this apparent problem to its advantage. Guaranteeing lifetime employment allowed it to establish rigorous performance management processes and create the conditions for continuous improvement. The organisational culture that exists at Toyota today is the product of this long evolution.

So lean is much more than a combination of tools, methods and principles. The mindset and behaviour of the people operating the system are fundamental. Toyota's ability to align these intangible factors with its operating system is probably the aspect of its success that is most often overlooked; yet it is a key source of advantage. It is precisely this interdependency between structural and organisational features on the one hand and human aspects on the other that makes lean one of the most difficult management techniques to apply.

Our aim in writing this book is to help managers embark on the journey towards a truly lean system. Having witnessed at first hand the tremendous impact it can make on the bottom line, and the profound changes it can achieve in the motivation and effectiveness of managers and front-line staff, we hope to convince you that the journey is an exciting one.

Stefan Roggenhofer

Before I joined Toyota's UK plant at Burnaston in 1991, I'd heard a lot about the company's reputation for excellence. After a few weeks, I travelled to Japan to be inducted by the world-renowned operations management consulting division, the part of Toyota that created and continues to develop the Toyota Production System. I found the theory behind lean tools and methods logical and compelling, but it was their impact that most impressed me: very high productivity, very short lead times and exceptional product quality.

Returning to the United Kingdom as a technical specialist, I was involved in introducing the Toyota Production System to Europe. We started with a number of suppliers that were keen to build a relationship with Toyota and had offered to undertake pilot programmes. As soon as we started working with them, we were able to diagnose areas of waste and inefficiency in their operations and put corrective measures in place. The managers were astounded: within a few days, we had achieved far more than any previous improvement programme, and at almost zero cost. It looked like a miracle: huge improvements in labour productivity, inventory and quality, and all for free.

But the euphoria soon faded. When we returned to the sites a few weeks later, it was business as usual. Extra people were back on the line, inventory levels had soared and quality problems were slipping through once again. When we asked management why they had allowed performance to deteriorate, they were incredulous; most hadn't even realised that gains had been eroded. So we set about helping them to rebuild the system. But by our next visit, performance had again slumped back to the old level.

So what had gone wrong? Weren't the suppliers committed? Were they merely playing lip service to a major customer? Or was their management to blame? In the end, we managed to put things right, but it took a long time and extraordinary efforts to re-establish what had originally been achieved in a matter of days.

Our experience was far from unique. For all the energy that companies have invested in implementing lean over the past 20 years, the rewards have often proved to be short lived. What was missing? What was the secret ingredient that would help to deliver impact combined with sustainability? Those were the questions I tried to answer; you'll find the conclusions I have drawn within these pages.

Blair McCallum

Working in manufacturing for a number of years has taught me that operational improvement work must be done *through* people, rather than to people. I've also learned that people are seldom persuaded to change the way they work because of a manual, a presentation or a briefing. Of course, logical explanations and clear instructions have their place, but they must be backed up by practical demonstrations. People need proof that a new approach works: 'I'll believe it when I see it.'

Now, as a consultant working at the interface between operational and behavioural change, I find that sharing our experience of changing mind-sets and behaviours with managers is difficult. Written documents and conventional presentations aren't that helpful. They can do a good job of explaining the theory underpinning lean operations, but they can't give people an understanding of what lean feels like, of the difference it makes in their everyday working lives.

So why then write a book about lean operations? The answer is that we have tried to do two different things in this book. In Part I, The Lean Landscape, we have provided a structured introduction to the aspects that any company contemplating a lean transformation will need to work on. In Part II, The Lean Journey, we portray the transition to lean operations from the point of view of a company involved in the messy reality of everyday operations. This part takes the form of a drama documentary, with events interspersed with commentary and analysis. We hope readers will be able to engage with Arboria's management team and front-line workers as they grapple with the problems and frustrations of implementing lean, and glimpse the rewards it offers. That way, they can start to experience a little of this challenging yet rewarding journey for themselves.

John Drew

CHAPTER 1

The Challenge of Lean

- ■ Lean can transform operations in any sector, opening up new strategic opportunities.

- ■ Lean is far more than a set of tools; it is a radically different way of working.

- ■ Implementing lean is a journey, not a process.

Excellence is inspiring. Watching Tiger Woods can spur us to dust off our golf clubs and get down to our local course. Full of good intentions, we promise we'll go the full 18 holes, work on our handicap and spend more time on the green and less in the bar. We may even sign up for lessons with a pro, or splash out on a new set of clubs in the hope they will lift our game.

But we all know that good intentions aren't enough. Once the initial rush of enthusiasm has subsided, we need to follow through with determination and sheer hard work. Time after time, we find that achieving our goals is much harder than we ever imagined.

It's just the same for corporations and their improvement programmes. Often inspired by Japanese car makers, countless companies throughout the world have endeavoured to boost their performance by adopting a lean approach, changing shop-floor practices to eliminate waste from their operations. But for the vast majority, improvements have been short lived. Any gains they have won came at the expense of special efforts and additional resources. As soon as managers let up, even for a moment, the improvements vanish into thin air.

Part of the reason is that shop floors tend to be unpredictable places. Such is the habitual state of any system; nature prefers chaos. No improvement can be sustained unless effort is put into maintaining it. Indeed, in a highly unpredictable environment, so much effort is needed merely to maintain the status quo that doing work to improve the process is out of the question. As one manager put it, implementing change in such conditions is 'like trying to pitch a tent in a hurricane'. The challenge is all the more acute when the responsibility for quality, cost and delivery to the customer is delegated down the organisation to managers at the front line.

Having worked closely with many managers on improvement initiatives as well as having worked in industry ourselves, we are under no illusion about the difficulty of achieving sustainable change. Firefighting is the norm in many organisations, and is a symptom of an operation that is fundamentally unstable. Such instability is an inevitable characteristic of mass production.

Even when sophisticated scheduling systems such as manufacturing requirements planning (MRP) are in place, the vagaries of demand and supply virtually guarantee that the two are continually out of synch. The problem lies with the notion of scheduling itself: people are never willing or able to comply with schedules for long. Customers change their orders at the last minute, deliveries don't arrive on time, parts run out, and machines break down. As soon as a problem arises, scheduling is likely to go awry, and operators have to be creative and cut corners to keep production running.

Though well intentioned, these unplanned interventions compound the problem. Relatively small deviations at a given stage in the process can quickly be amplified to create wild fluctuations in supply and demand along the value chain. It's no accident that the central planning of the old Soviet economy failed catastrophically. Scheduling relies on compliance and predictability, but no operation ever runs that smoothly.

This leaves us with a conundrum. If variability is inherent in mass production and if it inevitably leads to instability and fire fighting, can any change programme ever have lasting impact? Won't instability eventually blow down the tent of any new system as employees are forced to revert to the old ways of doing things?

Lean's Great Promise

Lean has entered management consciousness in a big way in recent years. No longer regarded as an arcane set of Japanese methods and tools, it appeals because it holds out a promise no other approach can make: not only does it cut costs and improve quality, but it also stabilises operations and matches supply with demand. It even promises to end firefighting for good and establish the necessary conditions for continuous improvement.

When lean becomes a way of life rather than a project, it can make an enormous impact, surpassing managers' expectations and conferring enormous competitive advantage. By applying lean principles, Dell turned over its inventory 64 times in 2001, 50 times more than its nearest rival, while incurring operating costs that were less than half those of its closes competitor. Dell's founder, Michael Dell, says the principles of its success are simple: 'What's the point in having a monitor put on a truck to Austin, Texas, and then taken off the truck and sent on a little tour around the warehouse, only to be put back on another truck? That's just a big waste of time and money.'

Many other companies have made the same transition. By adopting lean principles, Airbus UK, which manufactures wings for assembly at plants in France and Germany, was able to release substantial latent capacity that obviated the need for major capital expenditure. By 1999, an extended period of demand growth was creating severe capacity constraints, and Airbus was experiencing increasing difficulty in meeting performance targets. Adherence to schedules was critical, since missed delivery dates to partner companies incurred financial penalties.

Airbus UK started its transformation in two pilot areas: machining and single-aisle wing assembly. In the machine shop, the adoption of lean methods boosted internal schedule adherence from around 30 per cent to over 75 per cent in three months. In assembly, new production methods and logistics systems delivered productivity savings of more than 25 per cent, a reduction in production cycle time of around 20 per cent, and improvements in quality of over 40 per cent within six months. By 2003, the company had achieved impressive results: 100 per cent delivery on schedule, with less recourse to outsourcing; productivity up by over 25 per cent; minor quality issues down by over 50 per cent. Airbus UK is now recognised as one of the top performing business units within Airbus.

The US insurer Jefferson Pilot Financial (JPF) is another company that has achieved radical improvements in performance by applying lean principles.[1] In late 2000, JPF began looking for ways to break free from the slow growth that characterises the life insurance industry. The challenges it faced were daunting. Product proliferation, driven by rising customer expectations, was ratcheting up complexity and costs for full-service players. At the same time, specialist niche players boasting lower costs and faster policy handling were creating unprecedented pressure to improve service levels *and* cut costs.

Jefferson Pilot was among the first to realise that lean principles and tools could be applied to the processes of a financial services company.

---

1   See Cynthia Karen Swank, 'The lean service machine', *Harvard Business Review*, October 2003.

brought it substantial gains: the time it took to turn around
on fell by 70 per cent, the labour cost per policy by nearly
d the number of policies reissued due to error by 40 per cent.
European telecommunications provider successfully applied
er pressure on its margins in a regulated and slowing market.
tially on an area that was prompting many customers to switch
to other providers: the repair of faults in fixed lines.

The team found that the three stages in the repair process – call centre, diagnosis and field force – operated in such a disconnected way that they were like three rival companies. They even worked different hours. The result was an average repair time of roughly 19 hours, of which only about an hour was work that benefited the customer. Some 20 per cent of the field force's time was spent waiting for work to be allocated, for instance, and another 20 per cent went on travelling between jobs.

By using lean principles first to find the leaks in the value stream, and then to realign the organisation and invest in team leaders, the telecoms company achieved impressive results. In the first few months of the pilot, productivity rose by 40 per cent, and the rate of recurring failures fell by 50 per cent. This success was subsequently replicated across the company's entire national network. What began as a productivity improvement programme ended as a veritable cultural transformation. As the COO put it, 'We have surpassed the goals of this programme. The most important success is that the organisation has learned and grown. It is now implementing on its own.'

We will return to these examples in later chapters to show how lean can transform operations in any industry. We have seen businesses from many sectors – chemicals, paper, mining, steel, consumer goods, pharmaceuticals, retail and financial institutions – reap rewards by applying lean to their operations.

Toyota: The Lean Pioneer

Such companies are applying ideas first introduced by Toyota, the founder of lean. Toyota's approach to manufacturing has enabled it to earn higher profits and sustain faster growth than any of its competitors over the past 30 years, with total return to shareholders increasing at a compound annual growth rate of 14 per cent. By 2003, Toyota was the world's third largest automobile manufacturer, with a global market share of just over 10 per cent, up from 5 per cent in 1970. It recently announced its aim to increase this share to 15 per cent by 2010. If it succeeds, it will become the biggest car maker in the world.

Even in today's difficult climate, Toyota achieved a return on sales of 8 per cent in 2003. Yet it isn't known as a pioneer of innovative products, or a cutting-edge market strategist. Rather, the key to its success is the world's most efficient operating system: the Toyota Production System.

Toyota's journey to lean started when it began to develop new operating principles in response to the business challenges it faced in the Japan of the 1950s. Following the destruction of the country's economy in the Second World War, capital was scarce, limiting access to corporate finance. Low incomes meant the home market for cars was tiny, so Toyota didn't have the scale of demand to justify mass production. Moreover, its models were yet to be tried and tested, so heavy investment in tooling up was out of the question. And the company needed to cut costs, but was prevented from laying off workers by stringent legislation introduced to protect employment. Its attempts to improve efficiency met only with strikes and deteriorating industrial relations.

A lesser company might well have given up at this point. But this inauspicious set of circumstances was the impetus for Toyota to develop a more flexible production process that would be less dependent on long production runs. To reduce capital costs, it purchased second-hand machinery from the United States. This lower level of investment meant that the small-batch production Toyota needed to satisfy its limited market was now theoretically feasible. The practical obstacle that stood in the way was the enormous cost and complexity of retooling machines to switch between multiple short runs. In mass production, retooling was a massive job that could involve closing down a line for days, retraining employees and even introducing new machines into the line.

So Toyota developed a production system that enabled frequent and rapid changeovers. Instead of using single-purpose machines, it introduced equipment that could take interchangeable tools. It worked on reducing the complexity of machine set-ups and the physical distance tools needed to be moved. Above all, it invested in its employees. They had to be able to change over tools when needed, to do a range of different jobs and to move from one line to another, so they had to be trained to much higher levels than usual. But Toyota knew the investment would pay for itself because the employees would stay with the company for a long time, perhaps their whole careers.

Having a highly skilled workforce brought a second benefit: the company was able to involve its staff in continually improving the changeover process. By shifting the balance of its investment away from capital equipment and towards people, it had found a way of increasing its flexibility. Toyota's short production runs now became a benefit rather than a burden, as it was able to respond much more rapidly to changes in demand by quickly switching production from one model to another.

Over time, all these elements were consolidated into a new approach to operations that formed the basis of what we now know as lean.[2] As this brief history suggests, lean is an alternative to mass production, not a complement to it. It calls for a completely different way of operating, and for a completely different way of *thinking* about operations. Lean is not compatible with large-batch production; instead the pace, mix and quantity of production is set by the customer. Mass producers set themselves limited goals: an acceptable number of defects, a tolerable level of inventories, and a narrow range of standardised products. Lean producers, on the other hand, aim for perfection: continually declining costs, zero defects, zero inventories and endless product variety.

What Toyota did was to develop an operating system that didn't depend on the economies of scale of the huge American market. Instead, it developed a culture, organisation and operating system that relentlessly pursue the elimination of waste, variability and inflexibility. To achieve this end, it focuses its operating system on responding to demand – and nothing else. This in turn means it has to be flexible; when there are changes in demand, the operating system must respond immediately. Underpinning the whole system is a stable workforce that is required to be much more skilled and much more flexible than those in most mass production systems. True flexibility requires stability; you can't have one without the other.

Toyota's operating system has made a virtue out of a necessity. All its key attributes can be traced back to the market conditions of the 1950s. But if Toyota developed lean as a response to a specific set of problems at a specific moment, can it be the answer for companies operating in today's very different conditions?

The current environment is in many ways diametrically opposed to that of 1950s Japan. Capital is abundant and global, so it seldom represents a source of competitive advantage, whether in terms of access to finance or manufacturing scale. Nor is it a barrier to entry: as memory-chip manufacturers found to their cost, competitors can spring up almost overnight, despite the amount of capital required. As a result, companies can't rely on scale to win market share. Moreover, if scale *isn't* a source of advantage, then mass production systems are a potential liability, not an asset.

---

2   See James P. Womack, Daniel T. Jones and Daniel Roos, *The Machine That Changed The World*, New York: Rawson Associates, 1990.

The uncertainty of today's globalised economy demands an agile operating system that is able to respond to rapid shifts in demand and changes in taste. The last thing a company wants is an inflexible production system that relies on shed-loads of inventory to protect it from changes in demand and market conditions, and that is about as manoeuvrable as an oil tanker on the high seas.

So we would argue that the flexibility of the Toyota Production System makes it well suited to the current economic environment. Indeed, it has become a powerful asset for its originator. Toyota's very short production runs are able to marry high quality with abundant product variety – a combination that is otherwise difficult to achieve and appears to bewilder competitors as much as it pleases customers.

The challenge that other companies face in adopting lean principles is that Toyota's system has years of collective learning built into it. Lean systems are inherently knowledge-intensive. Much of this knowledge is captured within highly refined systems and processes, but a good deal more resides in the skills of the people who operate them. Toyota people have a Toyota mindset. They know how to respond and when to respond to changes in production.

It's revealing to look at the way Toyota handles its overseas operations. When it sets up production in a new country it doesn't expect to find a fully established local system of components supply. Lean has to be taught to its new suppliers one by one. So though the local Toyota factory might start out lean internally, it will not be as efficient, initially at least, as the plants in Japan. To achieve parity, its suppliers will have to be both lean and local.

At first, the company has to manage the batch delivery of components – either imported from Japan or bought in from local suppliers – to its new overseas factory. However, the resulting lower levels of efficiency don't deter the company from making such overseas investments because it knows that productivity will increase over time as it gradually spreads lean throughout its supply base. As it does so, component supply becomes more and more local.

Toyota treats each new overseas operation as the start of a new journey to lean. Despite its years of experience in running lean operations, it doesn't expect to reach its goal in a single bound.

A Difficult Journey

If lean is such a powerful approach and Toyota models it so well, why is it that so few companies are able to implement it successfully? We might just as well ask why we struggle to improve our golf handicap, even though it seems so worthwhile. Part of the reason, no doubt, is that the appeal of a better handicap fades as the task proves tougher than we had imagined. Time pressures get in the way, bad weather keeps us off the course, family commitments intervene, or more attractive opportunities come along to distract us. In much the same way, many companies' attempts to 'do lean' peter out before they ever take hold. Good intentions are swamped by day-to-day demands. Priorities change as the organisation responds to external pressures. This is why we look on lean as a journey. It calls for able leadership, a reliable vehicle, a skilled and enthusiastic crew, adequate supplies, a reliable map and frequent checks on progress along the way.

The journey to lean is not for the timid, and there are no stopping places along the way. You can't hope to reap half the benefits of lean by being half-hearted. Making the transition is highly challenging, and many fall by the wayside. You need to be completely committed before you set out.

A lean transformation should not be seen as a technical process that's best left to technical people. In our experience, most companies that try to replicate the success of lean role models fail because they don't see the whole picture. When visitors tour a Toyota plant, for example, they see a set of tools and techniques that optimise operations, but not the infrastructure and behaviours that support them.

It's rather like watching a play at the theatre. We see the actors move around and hear them speak, but we don't know what happened during rehearsals, what the director asked them to do, how they prepared for their parts, how the playwright revised the script, or how tonight's performance may differ from yesterday's or tomorrow's. Like a stage play, too, lean operations aren't static, but evolve dynamically over time.

Staying the course of the lean journey calls for strong leadership. All change programmes need the commitment of senior management if they are to succeed; for lean transformations, this is doubly so. Because lean is a radically different way of operating, few people will immediately understand it. Until they see its benefits for themselves, they may well react against it because it challenges and undermines customary practices such as accumulating inventory to protect against problems. Especially in the early stages, experienced operations managers in particular are likely to feel threatened as they see cherished ways of working overturned.

Senior management needs to share the vision not only for *what* is to be achieved, but *how*. People involved in the change need to be given a degree of security and support, especially if lean is introduced in the context of a radical reduction in costs. Many companies that have successfully introduced lean have provided some form of employment guarantee to the employees who remain after the initial reduction in labour that lean usually makes possible. Without such assurances, employees may suspect that lean principles are just another way of putting them out of a job – hardly an inducement for them to participate actively in the change process.

The journey to lean is also a long haul. If a company is to become fully lean, it must be able to keep up its efforts over time. Although lean does yield immediate results, the full benefits come only when it becomes the basis for a process of continuous improvement. Accommodating such a long-term perspective presents a challenge to modern businesses. Today's short-term focus on quarterly results, coupled with short tenures at senior level, indicates that lean can't be sustained by the willpower of individual senior managers alone. Companies need to institutionalise lean practices and perspectives as part of their capability building. In short, everyone in the organisation needs to think lean.

Setting Out on the Journey

Lean principles aren't intuitive; indeed, they run counter to the experience of most operations professionals. So a company embarking on a lean journey will need the support and guidance of people with substantial experience of lean implementation.

Some companies have hired directly from Toyota and other lean companies and nominated their new recruits as change agents. Whoever you choose to work with, the right people for the job will be those who have previously helped to design and introduce a lean operating system. Many claim to have designed a lean system, but few have successfully implemented a sustainable one.

The journey to lean is by its nature a collaboration in which everyone in the organisation will eventually have to play his or her part. Change agents and lean guides are facilitators of change, helping others to make the journey and develop lean expertise of their own. If the journey is successful, all those involved will find themselves achieving things they would never have thought themselves capable of.

For many managers, embracing lean means venturing into unknown territory. The same is true for front-line employees, but in a different way. Through their day-to-day experience on the shop floor or with customers, they know the operational landscape inside out: not the theory of how things should work, but what actually happens, what the problems are, and how to keep things running. Implementing lean will challenge the perceptions managers and shop-floor staff have of one another. Both must learn to trust each other much more than ever before.

Although the lean journey is different for every organisation, most companies travel through five phases.

First comes a preparatory phase in which leaders assess whether lean can deliver their operations strategy, and make an informed decision to embark on the journey.

In the next phase, companies explore the opportunity for improvement by conducting a comprehensive assessment of the current state of operations, including the management infrastructure and employees' motivations and perspectives.

The third phase involves managers in defining the desired future state, aligning around a shared vision and committing to achieving it.

One of the toughest parts of the journey, phase four consists of implementing a pilot to demonstrate change to managers and front-line employees, test the design of the future state, and refine it as necessary.

In the final phase, change must be embedded in and spread throughout the whole organisation as a platform for achieving continuous improvement in all operations.

Although it may be tempting to turn these phases into a project plan or a process to be followed, the reality of the journey isn't like that. There's no 'right' way to approach a lean transformation. It could take months or even years for the leaders of one company to decide to embark on the journey, whereas others might do so in weeks. Equally, the sequence of events often isn't as neat as we have suggested. In some cases, a clear picture of the future state of operations may not emerge until after the pilot implementation, rather than before it.

Our aim in this book is to investigate what lean operations are, and how they work. We'll show how a comprehensive lean transformation, properly implemented, can create value for shareholders and customers. We'll also show what it feels like to be part of a lean transformation, giving an insider's view of what can be a turbulent and uncomfortable, as well as challenging and rewarding, transition.

Part I of the book – The Lean Landscape – outlines the three key aspects of lean and shows how they fit together (Chapter 2), before examining each of them in more detail (Chapters 3, 4 and 5). Part II – The Lean Journey – documents the progress of a fictional company on the journey to lean, with a chapter devoted to each of the five phases (Chapters 6 to 10).

Parts I and II are self-contained and can be read separately or consecutively. For people who like to have a clear structure in which to anchor their thinking, it probably makes sense to understand the landscape before making the journey. If, on the other hand, you prefer to immerse yourself in new experiences and then reflect on them, the lean journey may be a better place to start.

Wherever you start from, enjoy the journey!

The Lean Landscape

CHAPTER 2

The Essence of Lean

- Lean is not a project, but an ongoing quest for perfection through the elimination of all sources of loss.

- Taken to its fullest extent, lean is as much a strategy as an approach to improving operations.

- Lean requires the integration of three elements: operating system, management infrastructure and mindsets and behaviours.

'Lean' has entered the everyday language of operations – so much so that a whole range of operational improvement processes are commonly labelled as lean. As a result, lean means different things to different people. Many associate lean with the production system invented at Toyota, but believe it is confined to the eradication of waste in order to cut cost. In fact, there is much more to lean than that.

Put simply, lean is an integrated set of principles, practices, tools and techniques designed to address the root causes of operational underperformance. It is a systematic approach to eliminating the sources of loss from entire value streams in order to close the gap between actual performance and the requirements of customers and shareholders. Its objective is to optimise cost, quality and delivery while improving safety. To meet this objective, it tries to eliminate three key sources of loss from the operating system: waste, variability and inflexibility.

Waste is anything that adds cost but not value. Traditionally, seven types of waste have been identified: overproduction, waiting, transportation, over-processing, inventory, motion and rework. (See the Appendix for a list of sources of loss with symptoms, possible causes and key tools and techniques.) An eighth category is often added: the failure to use people's skills and contributions to enhance the performance of any business process. Toyota cite overproduction as the worst type of waste, since it both causes and hides the other losses. Whenever any type of waste is found in an operation, it is a sign that unnecessary cost is being incurred.

Variability is any deviation from the standard that detracts from the quality of a service or product delivered to the customer. In raw materials, for example, variability can lead to the production of defective parts or to equipment failures. In skills, it can lead to productivity losses or process bottlenecks that prolong lead times.

Inflexibility is any barrier to meeting changing customer requirements that can be overcome without incurring extraordinary cost.[1] Imagine you go to a furniture store to choose a new sofa, and the retailer tells you delivery will take 12 weeks. Making the sofa probably takes 10 or 20 hours. The rest of the time results from inflexibility caused, for example, by waiting for parts to arrive or batches of cloth to be cut and dyed. If you are shopping in November and want your sofa by Christmas, you will probably decide to take your custom to another retailer that can supply it in time.

There are obvious links between the three objectives and the three sources of loss. Eliminating waste helps to reduce cost; eliminating variability improves quality; and eliminating inflexibility optimises delivery. But this is an oversimplification; in practice, the interrelationships between objectives and sources of loss are rather more complex.

A successful lean transformation programme is holistic in nature and addresses all three sources of loss simultaneously, no matter where they might be found within the organisation. Instead of optimising individual parts or processes, it seeks to improve the whole system.

In this chapter, we explain how a lean transformation works and examine what it requires of an organisation. We also point out the hidden dangers encountered by businesses that try to take shortcuts on the journey to lean.

Extracting Hidden Potential

Extracting the hidden value in a company's operations is like drilling for oil. Every company has unrealised operational potential that can be readily identified in principle, but often proves remarkably difficult to capture in practice. As with oil, the first step is to quantify the rewards and understand the peculiarities of the terrain. Once you know how much potential lies hidden and you have determined that extracting it is economic, you need a stable platform to bring it to the surface. It is the capability to design and

---

1   The emphasis on changing customer requirements is one of the features that distinguish the lean approach from other forms of operations improvement.

operate this platform that separates the winners from the also-rans in the field of operational change.

Our experience in many different sectors has convinced us that to develop an effective change platform, companies need to tackle three aspects of an organisation simultaneously: the operating system, the management infrastructure, and the mindsets and behaviours of the staff. They are like the three legs of a platform: all three need to be securely in place and linked to one another if it is not to fall over (see Figure 2.1).

Operating system. Properly understood in terms of its purpose rather than merely as a system of execution, an operating system is the way in which assets, resources and people are managed in order to create value and flow it to the customer. An ideal configuration optimises the flow and minimises losses. In manufacturing, the operating system includes standard procedures, production control methods, process layout, equipment utilisation, inventory and manning levels. In a service industry such as banking, the components include information flows, IT systems, procedures and office layout.

Management infrastructure. Management processes, capability-building mechanisms and organisation structure need to be closely aligned with the

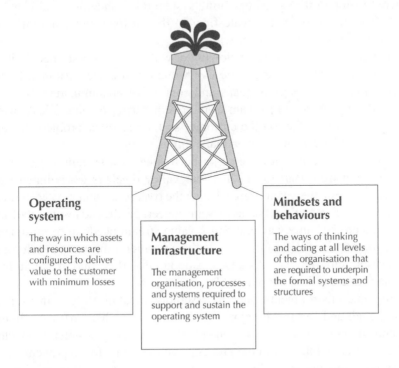

Operating system

The way in which assets and resources are configured to deliver value to the customer with minimum losses

Management infrastructure

The management organisation, processes and systems required to support and sustain the operating system

Mindsets and behaviours

The ways of thinking and acting at all levels of the organisation that are required to underpin the formal systems and structures

Figure 2.1 The three aspects of sustainable operational improvement

operating system so that lean ways of working become standard practice, not something that requires heroic efforts or exceptional teamwork. The entire management infrastructure must be designed to complement and sustain the operating system so as to achieve a high level of performance and foster an ethic of continuous improvement.

Mindsets and behaviours. The way people think about what they do, their attitudes towards their work, their aspirations and goals, and the effect these factors have on their actions need to be consistent with lean principles if improvement efforts aren't to unravel in the long run. It's imperative to engage people's hearts and minds: to ensure that staff at every level of the organisation understand the reason for change, know where it is heading, and commit themselves to working to get there.

Provided these three elements are linked together into an integrated whole, the change platform will be durable and robust.

The Operating System

The operating system lies at the heart of a lean company. It's the vehicle for adding value for the customer, and everything else in the organisation is there to support it. A good operating system takes an end-to-end view of a value stream in order to create flow to the customer and minimises the sources of loss that can occur within it.

Imagine a stream of water flowing downhill, with thirsty people in the valley below. This is like the flow of value towards the customer. In both cases, there are obstacles, leaks and sources of contamination along the way. If work is done upstream to remove a barrier or plug a leak, it will have negligible effect on the customer so long as other problems hamper the flow; indeed, it might even make things worse.

So the operations flow needs to be treated as a system – a complete progression from start to finish. If our valley dwellers get polluted water instead of fresh, they won't care whether the river was contaminated at source or in the last few yards. As far as they are concerned, the end result is the same.

In much the same way, the entire value stream needs to be completely pure to optimise the flow of value to the customer. Eliminating each source of waste will remove blockages, smooth the flow and make it more manageable and less unpredictable.

In some environments, such as assembly, creating flow is in itself the main goal, and can yield major improvements. In others, particularly bulk chemicals, consumer goods and other high-volume, capital-intensive sectors, flow is already inherent in the process, and the scope for improvement lies in eliminating losses.

The operations flow shouldn't be thought of as fixed. An organisation may well need to adapt it in order to cope with customers' changing demands. To take a simple example, a bank branch has to cope with peaks and troughs in customer demand throughout the day while at the same time maintaining service levels and productivity.

Management Infrastructure

The right management infrastructure will reinforce the lean operating system and ensure that performance objectives can be achieved and sustained. What the 'right' management infrastructure is will depend on the operating system it is intended to support; there is no universal solution that can be applied to every company.

Each element of the infrastructure needs to be tailored to fit the demands of the lean programme. Take the structure of the organisation: its design will involve decisions about team size, leadership, levels of hierarchy and the allocation of functional support. The criteria managers use in making these decisions will depend on the nature of the operating system. Complex processes generally call for small front-line teams with narrow spans of control. So do complex departments with unstable processes or poorly trained subordinates. A function such as maintenance should be integrated into a value stream if unplanned line stops are frequent. Planned maintenance, on the other hand, may need to be shared between multiple value streams, particularly if it draws on scarce specialist skills.

Similarly, performance management processes must be designed to ensure that employees have clear, measurable targets aligned with overall business objectives, and that performance against these targets is tracked in a completely transparent manner.

Airbus UK supported its lean transformation by strengthening management systems throughout its plant at Broughton in Cheshire. It focused on creating a new performance management system and redefining roles and responsibilities. Team-based performance targets were used to encourage cooperation among production employees both within and between shifts. In addition, clear service-level agreements were established to improve the performance of support functions such as logistics, quality, engineering and site maintenance.

For a lean operating system to bear fruit, front-line staff will need the skills and tools to track and manage operating performance. These must be embedded as a routine part of the organisation so as to link front-line activities to business objectives and set in motion the learning cycle that drives improved performance. Simple procedures such as holding a short team meeting around a performance board at the start of every shift can be much more powerful than any number of analyses and written reports.

Once an organisation has achieved a step-change in performance through lean, it enters a phase of continuous improvement that requires its own infrastructure. The nature of this infrastructure will change over time. Early on, substantial support will be needed at plant level. Later in the lean journey, the skills required to maintain the improvement programme will be transferred to the front line, and a smaller central team will be needed to act as guardians of the approach and developers of core materials and resources.

Mindsets and Behaviours

In any organisation, whether or not change sticks has a lot to do with how those involved perceive it. Do they trust their leaders and feel motivated, or fear for their jobs and suspect management is out to get them? Few managers are used to thinking about employees' mindsets, since they are hidden from view and hard to understand and influence. To work on them effectively calls for a set of skills that may not form part of the usual management repertoire.

The mindsets and behaviours of staff – or organisational culture – help determine whether changes can be sustained over time. Just as work must be done to develop the future operating system and management infra-structure, so effort must be devoted to defining and developing the behavioural state that will support them.

A lean operating system usually defines standard ways of carrying out certain tasks, for instance. These standards ensure that work is carried out safely, consistently and productively, and act as the basis for labour plan-ning. If they are to be implemented successfully, front-line employees will need to respect them and comply with them in a disciplined way. And if the standards are to be fully effective in the long term, employees need to be able to use their experience to help refine them to meet changing circumstances.

This can present a challenge to middle managers. Issuing instructions won't be enough; rather, they will need to act as coaches to help their teams make the move to the new way of working. But many front-line managers find coaching an alien concept. Among other things, they must learn to welcome the identification of problems, rather than punish those who point them out.

Such changes don't happen overnight. Indeed, they won't happen at all without strong leadership. The senior team must shape the culture by setting expectations about employees' behaviour. In any organisation, most people take their cue from those with power and influence, and are much more likely to modify their behaviour if they see change being modelled by those at the top. For this to work employees need to see their leaders on a regular basis; part of the lean challenge is that senior management must be much closer to front-line operations than ever before.

At Jefferson Pilot, the highly visible participation and commitment of senior leaders was key to the success of the lean transformation. The head of operations took part in periodic walk-throughs of the new process, and the vice-presidents were active in redesigning it. Their behaviour served to reinforce the importance of the effort and paved the way for its wider acceptance within the organisation.

Helping shape employees' outlook on their work is an important activity for managers undertaking any lean journey. If people aren't convinced that the extra trouble they have been put to is valued, they are unlikely to perform well. Managers who want their employees to engage in the change effort must first be willing to engage with them. This calls for a dialogue that explores employees' feelings about the change, including any frustration or scepticism. What surfaces during the dialogue should not be dismissed as carping, but should be translated into positive action, with employees encouraged to help devise solutions to the issues they raise.

There are No Shortcuts

Most lean programmes include three ingredients: *kaizen* (Japanese for continuous improvement) workshops, benchmarking visits and the recruitment of employees from successful lean companies. Although all three can make valuable contributions, they need to form part of an integrated transformation programme to succeed. Wrongly applied, they can cause damage and lead to disappointment and cynicism.

Taken in isolation, each has its drawbacks. Workshops teach tools and techniques rather than help create a company-wide system for running a business. In benchmarking visits, observers tend to see only the physical aspects of lean operations; the underlying principles remain hidden and unexplained. And people who have worked in a lean environment don't necessarily know how to create one.

Let's look at each ingredient in turn.

Kaizen Workshops

Imagine a simple business system with six process steps. A typical *kaizen* workshop would focus on just one of these steps, and seek to make a dramatic change in it through a focused effort over a week or two. A multi-disciplinary team would be assembled specifically for the workshop. They would look for inefficiencies (too many people, excess stock, problems with quality) and suggest changes that could be carried out quickly using a 'just do it' approach.

By drawing together a handful of people from various functions for a short period of intense activity, such workshops create a temporary organisational form focused on a single narrow task. When the workshop members go back to their everyday jobs, the process operators – the people actually responsible for implementation – lose the support they need. None of the business systems have really changed, and the process quickly reverts to its former state.

Benchmark Visits

In our experience, it can be very difficult to make sense of what you see on a benchmark visit. Take a tool such as *kanban*. (For more on *kanban*, see Chapter 3.) You may know that the *kanban* is designed to trigger upstream production and delivery, but what you see is simply a small card attached to a box of parts. What you don't see is how the flow through the operating system is regulated.

Benchmark visits can't give you a complete understanding of all the technical aspects of the system, let alone show you how people's roles and responsibilities are defined, how they approach tasks, or what attitude of mind they need to perform them consistently. Moreover, a visit is just a snapshot, not a moving picture. It can't show you how things got to be this way, or how they are likely to change over time.

Lean practices are not things that can be copied from one place and pasted into another. A lean system is more like a living body than an inanimate object. It links all the various parts of an operating system into a coherent whole. This is why isolated lean initiatives so often fail. For managers who are keen to transplant the practices they have seen on benchmarking visits into their own organisation, it's frustrating to discover that their efforts have no lasting impact.

Recruitment from Lean Companies

Employees with hands-on experience of lean operations tend to come from production environments. They are often production operators or team leaders in companies with great pedigrees. Though they possess relevant knowledge and expertise, what they know best is how to carry out a lean operation as part of an integrated process. Very few know how to set about modifying a value stream or business system to enable a new way of working, or have experience of putting in place the infrastructure to support and sustain a business system. It's a mistake to expect builders to act as architects.

The idea of recruiting from lean companies is part of a now widespread tendency to approach operations improvement from the bottom up. This may be a reaction to the laborious top-down programmes of 10 or 15 years ago such as TQM (total quality management), which began with the CEO and filtered slowly down through the hierarchy to the rest of the organisation. Starting from the shop floor probably seems like a better bet to managers tired of waiting for real bottom-line business benefits to flow from these top-down programmes.

What's often missing from the newer bottom-up approaches, though, is the right perspective, level of support and infrastructure to ensure that practical changes can be sustained. Imagine you reconfigure a production line to minimise the space it takes up. You may then be able to hold only a very small amount of line-side stock. But if your whole logistics system is still geared up to deliver components weekly in pallet-loads, you'll soon be in chaos. Failures such as this all stems from a lack of understanding of what the transformation from a traditional operating system to a lean operation actually involves.

Lean as an Integrated Approach

It simply isn't possible to close the gap between your actual performance and what your customers and shareholders require just by improving the physical aspects of your operations. True lean programmes challenge the organisational structures and formal management processes that surround operations. They seek to diagnose and tackle cultural and behavioural barriers to change both on the shop floor and in the management suite.

Imagine that a supermarket sets up a team to improve the way it goes about filling shelves so that it can free up more time for serving customers. What will it take to create sustainable change?

In terms of the operation itself, what is needed is a clearly defined shelf-filling process, supported by simple standards and practical training. In terms of management infrastructure, the team may decide to add visual tools such as a magnetic board with coloured counters that tracks who is working on which tasks and acts as a guide to decisions on labour allocation. A few key indicators – say, cases handled per hour and time taken to unload a delivery – can be tracked on a daily basis and discussed during a brief team meeting every morning to review performance and agree priorities for the day ahead.

Finally, staff will need to be engaged with the effort from the start so that they understand the reasons behind it and know what will happen and what roles they will be expected to play. As the work progresses, it's vital that front-line staff derive their own benefits from the new way of working, perhaps by being able to spend more time with customers and less time behind the scenes performing mundane tasks or dealing with unplanned events. If staff don't benefit, management is unlikely to sustain the extra commitment and involvement that will be needed to make lean work.

The way that people think and act and the systems within which they work need to change at the same time. If systems don't change to address the root causes of operational problems, people will quickly become frustrated by the gulf between what they are being asked to do and the reality of their everyday experience. On the other hand, if the operating system and management infrastructure have been redesigned but people aren't fully engaged with the effort, any improvements will eventually unravel.

As we have shown in this chapter, our approach to lean transformation is to create a stable change platform by working on all three elements of the business simultaneously: operating system, management infrastructure and mindsets and behaviours. A failure to take account of any one of these is not just inadvisable but impossible, since working on one dimension will have a knock-on effect on the other two, leading to an unstable change platform.

In the next three chapters, we explore these three features of the lean landscape in more detail.

CHAPTER 3

The Lean Operating System

- A lean operating system follows certain principles to flow value to the customer while minimising all forms of loss.

- Each value stream within the operating system must be optimised individually from end to end.

- Lean tools and techniques are applied selectively to eliminate the three sources of loss: waste, variability and inflexibility.

On a recent visit to a factory, the operations manager told us that the company had 'done lean' a few years ago. The results had been great at first, but people had gradually reverted to their old way of doing things and the benefits had slipped away. This is a pattern we see repeated all too often.

The effectiveness of the lean operating system comes from the integrated nature of its practices and methods. Yet many organisations assume they can accomplish a lean transformation merely by applying a few lean tools. Not so. Such attempts are doomed to failure because there is no lean operating *system* in place to coordinate and drive improvements.

One company we know devoted its efforts to changeover reduction (SMED)[1] across its entire operation; another sought to apply the principles of workplace organisation (5S) as the basis for its improvement effort. The problem with such approaches is twofold. First, lean tools are being applied without reference to business needs. Second, they are being used outside the context of a coherent operating system that can enable the organisation to meet these needs.

For most companies, their operating system evolves haphazardly as their business grows. Imagine an entrepreneur who sets up a small bakery. She has few assets (just her premises, a mixing machine and an oven) and few resources or people to organise. Without realising it, she

---

1   Single Minute Exchange of Dies.

probably has a fairly lean operating system. It's flexible, and there is little waste.

Now imagine that because this woman's bread is very good, the business begins to grow, and she decides to invest in automated equipment to satisfy demand. Things go well, and after a while her bankers lend her the money to buy a run-down bakery. A few years later, the business has developed into a medium-sized business with several sites, a range of products, thousands of customers and hundreds of employees.

Whereas configuring assets and resources was once a simple matter (there are only so many ways to arrange an oven and a mixer), it has now become quite complicated. Once the woman received a few phone calls in the afternoon that enabled her to plan her production for the following morning; now she relies on other people and an IT system to tell her what she needs to make. Before, she had just one van that she drove herself; today she has a fleet of trucks that deliver fresh bread and other products to a range of outlets.

A growing business like this will probably see the main operating question it faces as 'How do we continue to satisfy growing demand at minimum cost?' Seldom does a management team in this situation have the time or skills to ensure that new capacity is added in a coherent way. For the most part, the configuration of assets, resources and people just happens; it is by accident rather than design.

Lean by Design

Our bakery example illustrated how a simple operation can be lean by accident; we now turn to a complex operation that became lean by design. We have already touched on the Toyota Production System (TPS), the first – and still the pre-eminent – example of lean. Many books have been written on its history, distinctiveness and influence, and we don't propose to replicate their findings here. But it does deserve further attention, for two reasons. First, it has stood the test of time, having delivered superior performance over almost half a century. Second, it offers useful lessons for companies operating in sectors other than automotive manufacture.

The Toyota Production System has three key elements: Just-in-Time production, Autonomation (a transliteration of the Japanese *Jidoka*, or 'automation with a human touch') and flexible staffing systems.

Just-In-Time Production

The objective of Just-in-Time production is to produce and transport just what is needed, just when it is needed, in just the amount needed, within the shortest possible lead time.

Many companies claim to respond to their customers 'just in time' when what they are actually doing is holding extra stock in order to meet customers' orders faster than their competitors can in the hope of gaining market share. This is a risky strategy. It incurs an inventory-holding cost and a consequent risk of obsolescence; it also fails to display true responsiveness to customer demand. Far from embracing lean, these companies are missing the whole point, substantially increasing waste rather than minimising it.

True Just-in-Time capability is achieved when the products delivered have actually been *manufactured* in response to customer demand, not just delivered from stock. The process holds the smallest amount of stock needed to meet the delivery lead times customers require, thereby minimising the waste associated with inventory, reducing the risk of obsolescence, and providing a much more responsive system. In practice, inventory needs to be seen as the lubricant needed to ensure that the system keeps flowing.

In order to implement Just-in-Time production, a company must create continuous flow processing, match the rate of production to the rate of customer demand by means of *Takt*, and control production through a 'pull' system. These building blocks depend on the foundation of levelled production, which smoothes the workload over time. Let's look at each of these in turn.

LEVELLED PRODUCTION

In an ideal world, Toyota would build cars to order in exactly the sequence that it received the orders. The reality is that variable work content – or differences in the total amount of time it takes to build different products – makes this impossible and demands a compromise, which is achieved through production levelling. In production levelling, true demand is artificially smoothed within a production period in order to create a steady 'pull' rate and product mix.

Figure 3.1 shows production cycles for three cars, L, M and H, each with different work content. Product L is a basic 'low specification' model; product H is a high-specification vehicle with extras that require additional work, such as a sunroof and air conditioning; and product M is a mid-range model. Most manufacturers would group similar products into batches to capitalise on economies of scale; Toyota does the opposite. The reason is apparent from the left-hand graph in the figure. Creating a batch of product L will mean that the production line is under-loaded; conversely, producing a batch of product H will mean that people have to struggle to cope with the extra work.

Levelling products over time, as in the right-hand graph, smoothes out these differences in work content, just as a 'rolling average' graph smoothes out peaks and troughs in data. Such a method relies on standardised work and a highly skilled and adaptable workforce. To achieve this quality of workforce is no easy task, and attests to the crucial role played by management infrastructure in supporting the Toyota Production System.

From batch production ...   ... to levelled production

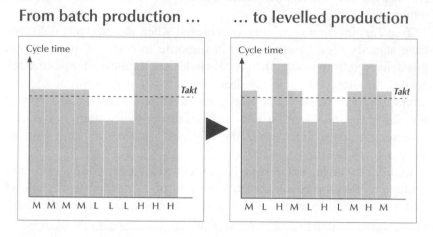

Figure 3.1 The smoothing effect of production levelling

As Figure 3.1 shows, levelling production normally increases the frequency of production of any one product, thereby allowing the total inventory to be reduced. Figure 3.2 explains this effect. Imagine that two products, A and B, are made on the same line. If product A runs for a week before changing over, then it follows that a safety stock of one week's worth of demand for product B must be held to ensure that the customer won't be left without any product. This leads to a minimum *average* stock level of roughly half a week.

Now imagine that production runs are reduced to a day rather than a week, as we see on the right-hand side of the exhibit. With each product made every other day, it's possible to satisfy customer demand while holding a maximum of just one day's worth of inventory. This represents a reduction in average inventory of about two-thirds. However, this outcome does depend on customer demand being steady. If there are spikes in the demand profile, some sort of buffer stock will be required.

From batch production ...   ... to levelled production

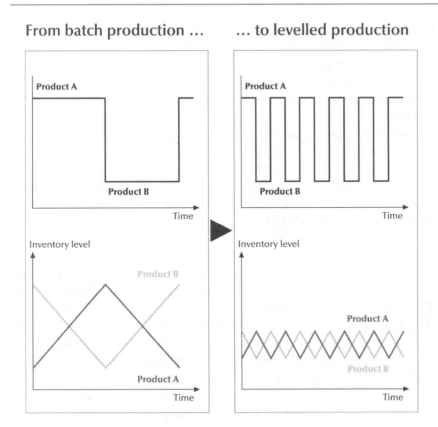

Figure 3.2 The impact on inventory

CONTINUOUS FLOW PROCESSING

In mass production, manufacturers have traditionally tended to organise their operations by grouping together similar processes to create 'process villages' that are geared to batch production. Within a machining shop, for example, lathes and mills are housed in two separate groups. Although such an arrangement makes it possible for one person to operate several similar machines, the product tends to collect and stagnate between processes. This blocks material flow, which causes uncontrolled work in progress (WIP) to accumulate and prolongs lead times. It also hinders communication between processes and increases the risk of quality problems that affect whole batches, since defects will be discovered only when the new batch is used in the downstream process.

The alternative solution developed and practised by Toyota is to dedicate equipment and functions to a particular product or product family (or 'value stream'). Wherever it is safe and feasible to do so, processes are located next to each other in the actual sequence of operation. An operator can then work on one piece at a time and see it through to completion, instead of processing a batch of many pieces in parallel. As well as being more motivating for the operator, this arrangement minimises inventory and lead times and makes it easier to reallocate people from one product to another.

Continuous flow processing – often in a parallel or U-shaped work cell – is inherently more flexible, more visual, and more efficient, since it eliminates unnecessary movement and enhances communication. These features also make managing the production team easier. Once 'flow lines' based on product groups have been created, the rate of production can be matched to customer demand.

TAKT TIME

Takt is the German term for the beat or rhythm of a piece of music. *Takt* time is defined as the total available time for production divided by the total customer demand for that period. Imagine an insurance company that is open for 50 weeks a year and 37.5 hours a week, and has a steady rate of sales of 75 000 policies a year. In this case, the Takt time is 90 seconds (total available time of 112 500 minutes divided by 75 000).

Takt time is designed to optimise material flow in pursuit of Just-in-Time delivery to the customer. To do this, it sets the pace of production at the rate of demand, thus eliminating the risk of overproduction, which Toyota

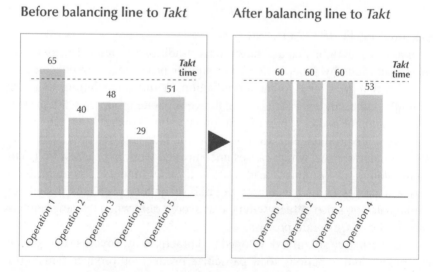

Figure 3.3 The productivity benefits of balancing to *Takt*

deems the worst type of waste since it hides (and also causes) other types of waste. Once an operation is working to a steady pace, it is much easier for management to monitor performance, allocate the labour force and plan capacity.

Takt time is used to balance work content in a continuous flow line, which often has the effect of reducing the amount of labour needed to build a product. Figure 3.3 illustrates the impact of balancing five workstations to a *Takt* time of 60 seconds. The normal approach is to balance all but one of the workstations to *Takt*, leaving the remaining workstation (Operation 4 in the figure) with a lower work content. In the short term, this spare capacity provides flexibility for dealing with any problems that occur during the production cycle. However, in the longer term, this remaining fraction of a complete work cycle becomes the focus for continuous improvement activity.

In many industries, customer demand varies significantly from period to period, so companies have to be able to cope with fluctuations. Although they can recalculate *Takt* time in each period to ensure that customer demand is always met, this will involve rebalancing lines and retraining people – a massive task in complex industries. Even Toyota confines itself to revising *Takt* no more than twice a year to ensure that changes are manageable.

PULL

The final element of Just-in-Time production is 'pull' scheduling. A 'push' system is one where companies build products or offer services without a firm customer order, in the expectation that demand for their offering will materialise. A 'pull' system produces only what customers (or downstream processes) actually want.

To synchronise a particular operation with customer requirements, the process 'pulls' raw materials from the upstream process using the principle of replenishment. This greatly reduces the need for central production planning. It also does away with the associated problems of reconciling stock and production data on an ongoing basis in order to maintain the integrity of the system.

Many of us experience the benefits of a pull system in everyday life without realising it. The small controlled stock of burgers in a fast-food restaurant is an obvious example. This stock is determined by parameters such as the rate of production, level of demand and agreed safety stock, and is fixed at a level that ensures customers receive fast service and the risk of food wastage is minimised. As a product is served to a customer, an order is generated to replace it with a fresh product. Pharmacies manage their stocks of drugs in much the same way.

Notably, it was a visit to a supermarket in the United States that triggered the development of pull systems at Toyota. A visitor from the company noticed that the retailer was replenishing only those products that had been taken off the shelves by customers – a method it had implemented to reduce wastage in perishable items. The Toyota employee recognised that such an approach could easily be adapted to reduce waste in a manufacturing environment.

There are many ways of applying pull systems, but the essence is that parts are produced only once a signal – a *kanban* – has been received from the downstream process. Usually this signal tells the upstream process either to replace a part that has been consumed in some way, as in the supermarket example ('make to stock'), or to build it as a response to demand ('make to order'). The exact configuration of the system will depend on a number of variables, such as the size and value of the components; the number of variants and level of demand for each one; the information lead times; and the shelf-life of the product.

Working in this way has the general effect of increasing the frequency and number of changeovers. This is why changeover reduction (or SMED) techniques form an intrinsic part of lean. The need to change over processes more frequently creates an incentive to reduce changeover times so that the proportion of time spent on changeovers doesn't rise. Indeed, in many cases, it is reduced. A good rule of thumb is that roughly 10 per cent of total processing time should be spent on changeovers.

Toyota uses pull systems to target the most serious form of waste: overproduction. Surplus inventory masks and compounds other forms of waste. Removing it puts equipment reliability at a premium. It is for this reason that approaches used to maximise the reliability and utilisation of equipment in a systematic way, such as Total Productive Maintenance (TPM) and Reliability-Centred Maintenance (RCM), are an intrinsic part of lean operating systems.

Pull systems have been successfully applied in many different contexts beyond the retail and automotive sectors we've examined here. Examples can be found in the aerospace, biomedical, electronics and process industries.

Autonomation

Autonomation is a process designed to allow a workforce to detect production problems quickly and resolve them decisively. Its objectives are to improve equipment reliability, enhance product quality and increase productivity. It consists of three elements: detect and stop, alert, and root-cause problem solving.

Detect and stop. Toyota found that the most effective method of detecting a fault or abnormality is to give the responsibility to the people who operate the process. They must have a good understanding of what the customer requires so that they can decide when a product or part has gone beyond the acceptable limits of the process. To help operators detect problems, Toyota employs visual standards and mistake-proofing (or *Poka-yoke*) techniques.

Poka-yoke techniques are used to prevent abnormalities occurring in the first place, and to stop a process automatically when an abnormality is identified. An everyday example can be found in cars with an automatic gearbox: the car cannot be started unless the gear lever is in neutral. Another means of detection is to monitor the production rate and compare the actual rate to the target, which is based on *Takt* time.

Once problems have been detected, the process should wherever possible be stopped. This can be done manually or – in cases where the stop mechanism is linked to the detection process – automatically. In process industries, it may not always be feasible to stop the process, but it is still important to detect the problem as quickly as possible so that corrective action can be taken. Such industries often use statistical process control to monitor the processes and detect when a problem has occurred.

Alert. Once a problem has been detected, the process or the operator needs to alert the team leader. This can be done verbally, by means of an *Andon* board (a display that indicates production status), or via an audible alert.

Root-cause problem solving. Even if it isn't possible to rectify the root cause immediately, it's important to take action to contain the problem before the process is restarted. It may be, for example, that an additional check needs to be made on every component until the source of an intermittent fault upstream in the process has been identified and addressed.

Flexible Staffing Systems

As Toyota strives to match its production to true customer demand, a point will come where the variation in demand for individual products will mean that certain flow lines are under utilised while others are over-burdened. At this point, managers will need to reallocate resources quickly as demand changes. The mechanism that enables them to do so is known as the flexible staffing system. Its objective is continuously to optimise labour productivity to whatever the level of demand may be.

In an assembly environment where the demand for different product lines is relatively predictable from one week to another, this is achieved by changing the *Takt* time of the lines involved and then dividing the total work content by the *Takt* time to determine the number of people required at this level of demand. In practice, the tasks an individual operator needs to perform may well vary as the *Takt* time changes. This is why standards (such as standard work sequence charts) are needed to define the precise role each person must play at a given level of demand.

Consider a manufacturing area that has two cells, A and B, building two different product groups. The processes are well documented, with standards for each task that are used as the basis for training. Operators are trained in both sets of processes so that they are able to work on either line. Demand for the two products varies, but when demand for line A's product is high, demand for line B's product tends to be low.

The team leaders have worked out a line balance for three levels of demand: low, normal and peak (Figure 3.4). They work with the production scheduling team to understand demand changes and agree *Takt* times on a week-by-week basis. As Figure 3.5 shows, this flexibility enables the two lines to be run at an optimum rate: the 11 operators are fully occupied but never overloaded, and customer demand is always met. There is no need to build excess stock to keep people busy in quiet periods, or to run overtime at peaks in demand.

This simple example also shows how standards underpin an effective operating system and are central to any flexible staffing system. Clearly defined work standards and a good understanding of the work content of each job are prerequisites if people are to be moved between cells to rebalance lines without creating confusion. This is one of the reasons why Toyota and other Japanese manufacturers emphasize the need to standardise operations and so create a foundation for flexibility.

One important manifestation of standardisation is the use of visual management to make the status of an operating facility obvious to management and workforce alike. This extends from the overall layout of a process within a site, which should follow a logical flow, through to the storage of frequently used tools on shadow boards. The ideal state of a visual factory can be summed up in the saying 'a place for everything and everything in its place'; it should be obvious at a glance whether operations are proceeding properly and where any anomalies lie. Such transparency makes it possible to give front-line workers the

	Line A	Line B
Work content	600	540
Takt time at normal demand	120	90
People required at normal demand	5	6
Takt time at peak demand	100	75
People required at peak demand	6	7.2*
Takt time at low demand	150	110
People required at low demand	4	4.9

* 0.2 of job can be covered by team leader

Figure 3.4 Matching people to demand

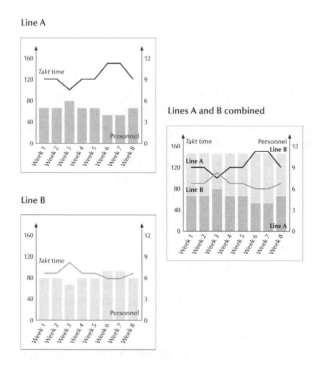

Figure 3.5 Adjusting staffing across two production lines to match demand

means and the responsibility to maintain the operating system in its correct state.

Employing visual management also engages the right side of the brain, which processes images and shapes holistically rather than analytically. People can *see* whether something has gone wrong much more quickly than they could diagnose it intellectually.

Having examined the key elements of the Toyota Production System, we now turn to the organising principles that characterise the lean operating system.

Core Principles of a Lean Operating System

Every business is unique. Any would-be lean company needs to design an operating system that takes account of its own particular context: its needs, assets, goals and so on. It is neither feasible nor desirable to copy an operating system from another organisation, or to attempt to follow some template or 'how to' guide. However, we have identified seven key imperatives that serve to sum up the distinguishing features of a lean operating system.

1: Create Value Streams by Grouping Similar Products or Services

So far, we have discussed value streams as though they already existed. In reality, a flow may be so haphazard and disconnected that the very notion of a value stream may appear meaningless. The first principle of a lean operating system, therefore, is that it is based on value streams that are created by grouping together similar products.

Exactly how the products should be grouped will depend on the business, but the criteria are likely to include patterns of demand, product characteristics and process routings. In many cases, the product and process criteria will define the value streams relatively easily. One manufacturer that made shock absorbers had two value streams based around two different technologies that required different equipment for the downstream half of the process.

In other cases, the product groupings will be less clear-cut. At one cosmetics factory, the operating system was reconfigured to create one value stream dedicated to steady products (even though there were many of them) and another for promotional products, whose demand characteristics were completely different. At Airbus UK, the value streams were defined as single-aisle, long-range and wide-body aircraft.

In a service industry, the task of identifying value streams calls for creative thinking. In a hotel, for example, value streams might be defined in terms of customer needs such as rest, food and beverages, and recreation. Such a grouping might then lead to changes in the design of processes and allocation of resources. It might be that the logistics supporting rest (such as laundry services) would be treated separately from the logistics supporting food and beverages (such as the ordering and delivery of meat).

The insurer Jefferson Pilot tackled this challenge by grouping together several related tasks, such as 'receiving and sorting' with 'system entry and routing'. Once it had established the value streams in this way, it determined the expected volumes that would be handled by each one.

2: Flow the Value Along the Stream from Beginning to End

Having established its value streams, a business then needs to design its operating system so as to ensure there is a flow of value to the customer from the start of the value stream to its end. In many cases, 'value' will mean a product such as a car or a loaf of bread. The value stream should be configured to enable this product to be ordered, manufactured and delivered to the customer within the shortest possible lead time.

In practical terms, this will mean dedicating equipment to a value stream wherever possible so that the flow isn't interrupted by the need to change to shared equipment. Whenever the value stream is broken, the execution of production processes is delayed and inventory increases. Though sharing equipment is sometimes unavoidable (as with especially expensive or complex machinery), it is more often the result of misguided attempts to cut unit cost, as opposed to optimising total cost. Sharing equipment carries costs of its own, as attested by the bottlenecks that emerge in any process using shared resources. Although dedicating equipment and resources to a single value stream may require a net increase in investment, it is often more cost-effective in the long run once the benefits of lower inventory, shorter lead times and fewer quality risks have been added to the equation.

Implicit in the principle of maintaining flow is the objective of minimising the leakages that can occur along the value stream. The challenge is to build an effective process through which value is added and leaks are eliminated. Consider the leakage caused by excess inventory in the value stream. It could be that operators are stockpiling inventory to compensate for the vagaries of an unreliable machine. If the machine is made much more reliable, they will no longer need to build up these excess stocks, and the leak will have been plugged.

Three types of flow combine to deliver products or services to the customer:

- **Material flow** is the route by which raw materials are transformed through various processes until they reach the hands of the customer.

- **Information flow** is the communication of customer requirements or orders along the supply chain. By instructing each process what to do next, it drives the business system to ensure that the right product or service arrives at the right place at the right time.

- **People flow** is the way that people move within and between processes. It includes the allocation of people to value streams and the way they use equipment within a value stream.

It is necessary, though often difficult, to optimise all three flows at once. Consider a telecommunications operator working to improve its process for repairing faulty phone lines. Complaints received at the call centre must be passed on to the teams who diagnose faults, plan the work and make the repairs. Ensuring the timely flow of this information and maintaining the integrity of the data is central to creating an effective end-to-end process.

The workload and routing of the field technicians who make the repairs – the people flow – is a key determinant of both the lead time to repair the fault and the productivity of the workforce. Materials must also flow efficiently to ensure that the field team always has the tools and components it needs to do the repairs and yet the business is not burdened with unnecessary stocks.

3: Pull Products at the Points where the Flow must be Broken

In some sectors, such as retail and assembly, it is inevitable that the flow of value will be broken at some points in the operation. Perhaps a process needs to make use of an expensive piece of equipment such as a paint plant that has to be shared between several value streams. Or perhaps the value stream is organised not around predetermined processes but around highly variable interactions between people, such as in renting a car. Such situations produce a less precise value stream whose flow is susceptible to random interruptions. The best way to minimise the losses associated with these interruptions is to govern the regulation of the flow by using 'pull'.

Imagine a painting process in which parts required by a number of downstream assembly lines are painted in batches in different colours. Clearly, it won't be possible to maintain a continuous flow to each line all the time. But we can minimise disruptions to the flow by setting up a simple pull system. It involves storing a defined quantity of painted parts after the paint process so that the assembly lines can take parts as they need them. Whenever they take a box of parts, a *kanban* attached to it is returned to the paint process. Once a predetermined number of these *kanban* have accumulated, the paint process changes over to paint parts to replace those that have been used up. This regulating mechanism is a simple and efficient way to determine when the process should change over, what it should make and in what quantities. It allows the process to maintain the supply of parts while minimising the stock that is held.

4: Flex the Operation to Match Customer Demand

The first three principles of lean operations have dealt with the broad theme of configuring assets and resources to create material flow. There remains the overriding question of how best to introduce the demands of the customer into the value stream in the first place. This is where the best lean operators excel and the weaker ones fall short. Creating flow doesn't in itself bring about a lean operating system because customer requirements aren't constant.

The real skill isn't so much to optimise the flows for a given customer requirement, but to create an operating system that is self-correcting and can adapt to customer requirements with the minimum allocation of resources and cost. A lean operator is able to do everything it takes to satisfy a customer without carrying out activities or introducing product features that add cost but no value. This requires an understanding of true customer requirements and a capability to flex the scale and pace of operations in order to follow the customer.

Just as the pull principle often translates into the tool of *kanban*, the principle of flexing an operation to match customer demand often translates into the concept of *Takt* time. Suppose a private hospital specialising in a particular operation has demand for 16 operations a day and that the operating theatre is open for 8 hours a day, then this gives a *Takt* time of 30 minutes. This means that assets (operating theatre, beds, equipment, surgical tools) and resources (doctors, nurses, administrators) should be organised and optimised to complete one operation every 30 minutes. Now let's suppose that during the winter months, the demand for this operation increases to 24 per day. The *Takt* time will drop to 20 minutes, and assets and resources will need to be reconfigured (and probably augmented) in order to achieve it.

In value streams that don't process discrete units or that process very large quantities, such as a chemicals plant or an oil refinery, the concept of *Takt* time will need modification. In a chemicals plant, for instance, the product mix needs to be managed to match demand as closely as possible even where the physical rate of production is determined by chemical processes or equipment considerations.

Strongly seasonal markets present a different kind of challenge. Take an ice-cream manufacturer. Its operating system must find ways of flexing production to accommodate the ebb and flow of customer demand. It may take on temporary workers at peak times, or enable its workforce to bank additional hours in the summer months that they can then take as holiday during the winter.

At a retail bank, the operating system will need to accommodate peaks in demand at lunchtimes. This will probably mean that multi-skilled members of staff will need to play a customer-facing role during these peak hours and revert to a back-office role at quieter times.

5: Introduce Information Defining Customer Requirements at a Single Point, and as Late as Possible in the Process

Managing operations through a centralised planning or scheduling function is much like managing a centrally controlled economy. It should work in theory, but in practice it seldom does because of the difficulty of managing variations in a timely fashion. Centralised systems rely on a few basic underlying assumptions. Once these are in any way challenged (because a delivery is late, or a batch of parts is defective, or a machine breaks down), the system quickly deteriorates, leading to a vicious cycle in which scheduling grows increasingly dependent on individual interventions instead of the central system.

Consider a simple manufacturing process that makes metal components for lawnmowers in three steps: pressing, welding and painting. Suppose that customer demand for a given day is 300 identical parts. A typical production control system would translate this requirement into a build list for each process. Suppose that, historically, pressing has operated with an average defect rate of 5 per cent, welding 10 per cent and painting 20 per cent. The production control system would issue an instruction to pressing to make 440 parts to ensure that 300 make it through to the customer (300 divided by the cumulative defect rate, 0.95 x 0.90 x 0.80).

However, the one thing you can always rely on is variability. On any given day, the defect rates may not be 5, 10 and 20 per cent, but perhaps 10, 10 and 25 per cent. In this example, only 267 parts would make it through to the end of the process: a shortfall of 33 parts. To increase the production target is *not* the answer; on another day with a different pattern of defect rates, starting with the requisite number of 440 parts could lead to a substantial surplus.

As this example illustrates, traditional production control systems tend to offset the risk of failing to meet customer demand by increasing batch sizes and adding buffer stocks. This adds cost and increases lead times. The complex conditions surrounding most production processes can only magnify the problem. As well as managing defect rates, the operating system must also take account of assumptions about such things as machine breakdowns and changeover times. As product and process complexity increases, the challenge of managing information flows gets steeper.

So how would a lean operating system differ? It seeks to introduce the information defining customer requirements into the system in such a way as to avoid the overproduction and shortages that plague centrally planned economies and mass producers alike. The key is to introduce the information at a single point local to the value stream, rather than at every point in the value stream or at some point remote from it, and then hard-wire all other processes to this information at the point of introduction, thereby establishing a physical connection between production and demand. This is possible because the *Takt* time governing the production rate is itself determined by actual demand.

Once the information defining customer requirements has been introduced, the system pulls the product or service through the value stream accordingly. The precise mechanism it uses will depend on whether operational lead times are longer or shorter than customer lead times. If shorter, products can be made to order; if longer, they must be made to stock.

Let's return to our example. Suppose that manufacturing lead times for lawnmower components are longer than customer lead times. In a lean system, we would need to hold a defined stock of finished products after the paint process. (These intermediary stocks needed to buffer production are called 'supermarkets' or 'shop stocks' and must be defined in terms of their location, quantity and replenishment method.) Today's demand is for 300 components of a particular design and colour, so this information is sent to the shop stock, where the parts are withdrawn and put on a truck to be delivered the customer. The withdrawal of these parts triggers a *kanban* to be sent to the paint process telling it to take 300 parts from the stock of unpainted parts and paint them to replace the components that have been sent to the customer, and so on up the value stream.

This method of production control eliminates the need to second-guess all sorts of uncertainties. If 20 parts should need to be scrapped from the paint batch of 300, then 20 replacement parts will be taken from the upstream shop stock, generating a signal to press an additional 20 parts to replenish this stock. In other words, the *actual* (and not the anticipated) demand is communicated up the value stream.

6: Standardise Operations to Create a Foundation for Flexibility

A common misconception is that lean is a highly standardised way of working that treats people like cogs in a machine and isn't suited to particularly complex or variable operations. On the contrary: rightly understood, standardisation is a necessary step in laying a foundation for true flexibility, and opens up opportunities for employees to develop new skills and enjoy greater variety in their work.

Consider the way ball boys and ball girls deal with variability on the tennis courts at Wimbledon. The 'customer demand' they serve – tennis balls that fall out of play – is inherently unpredictable, but they are able to cope with it by operating to a standard process that governs everything from their positions on the court to the way they retrieve and return the balls. Having been trained, they are given responsibility to make decisions for themselves rather than refer to authority. They are able to go about their business in the company of highly paid international tennis stars without distracting them or getting in the way.

It's a similar story in a lean environment, where standards create flexibility so long as the people who work to them are properly trained and have responsibility for maintaining them. Without this freedom of interpretation, standardisation can indeed become constricting.

Operating standards ensure that the safest and most efficient way of working is defined and repeated. This has benefits for customers, who will see better and more consistent quality; shareholders, who will gain from higher productivity; and employees, who have clear and safe procedures to follow. Standards also greatly reduce the risks associated with introducing new products or changing a process.

At the most basic level, standards ensure that tasks are done the same way no matter who is doing them. They also provide a foundation for training, and a baseline for improvement activity. They should be seen as living documents, constantly updated by work teams as they apply them. As processes are improved, standards need to be updated to capture the changed conditions, which then become a new baseline for improvement.

Whether they are to do with greeting a guest in a hotel, answering the telephone in a call centre, or building a car, standards assure the quality of an operation and thus protect the brand and the market premium it commands. They also play an important part in flexible labour systems by making it easier for individual employees to switch from one task or work cell to another. This enables companies to respond quickly to fluctuations in customer demand and thus maximise their productivity.

The use of visual management in the workplace also plays a vital role in building flexibility within the operating system. As well as making the location of materials and tools transparent, it can be used to create commonality between different work areas and between different sites, making it far easier to transfer people from one workplace to another.

7: Detect and Fix Abnormalities as Close as Possible to the Point Where They Occur

The final principle of a lean operating system has to do with quality management. At Toyota car plants, assembly workers are authorised to stop an entire production line if they find a defect that they can't resolve within the normal work cycle. In such a capital-intensive environment, the cost of not producing is extremely high, but Toyota has judged that the cost of producing defective products is higher still.

What's more, Toyota trusts its front-line workers to make judgement calls about what constitute quality problems. This is unusual; in most other companies, defects are handled in one of two ways. Either a group of people with special responsibility for quality is called in to investigate abnormalities and decide what to do, or else the news that a quality problem has occurred makes its way up the hierarchy until it reaches someone with the responsibility or courage to do something about it. In both cases, there is a substantial time lag between the detection of the problem and its resolution, during which the production of defective parts may well continue.

Contrast this with a lean operating system. Abnormalities are detected as soon as they occur, and if possible the process is stopped and not allowed to restart until the root cause of the problem has been identified and contained. This forces the organisation to institutionalise its problem-solving capabilities and pushes it towards continuous improvement. Such a rigorous process benefits customers by weeding out defective products and services, shortening lead times and reducing costs.

Putting it All Together

Because lean takes a holistic approach to the design of an operating system, it ensures that the root causes of underperformance, and not just the symptoms, are identified and treated. A business seeking to identify sources of loss will need to examine the whole operating system, from customers all the way back through the manufacturing processes to suppliers.

To understand this better, consider the case of a small sheet-metal fabricator that made parts for custom-built air-conditioning units. In an attempt to improve performance, its operations manager had already removed one bottleneck by replacing two old punches with a higher-capacity and more flexible new CNC punch. The process he was working on involved cutting sets of parts according to a job list. However, the sequence was often disrupted by a lack of the appropriate grade of metal.

After being cut, parts were stored and then moved to a workshop containing three folding machines. Although these folders had a sequence list to follow, they tended to cherry-pick jobs to suit the set-up of their machines. Deliveries to customers were consistently late.

The operations manager believed that the folding machines represented a bottleneck, so he ran some workshops to cut changeover times and help the folders work more closely to the sequence list. He was surprised to find this made no difference to delivery performance. Indeed, the folders often stood idle for long periods.

When the company took a step back and looked at the process in a more holistic way, from the supply of steel through to delivery to the customer, a different set of problems emerged. These related to the flow of information and the replenishment of sheet steel – the true sources of loss. Had the company identified them at the outset, it could have saved the £500 000 it invested in the new punch, and addressed customers' problems more quickly and directly.

Another manufacturer committed itself to constructing an expensive new workshop when it ran out of space. But a systems perspective revealed that most of the existing floor space was taken up by inventory. The weak points in the operating system turned out to be poor information flows as much as bottlenecks in material flows. Tackling them allowed the company to reduce inventory drastically within a few months. Had it done so earlier, it might never have needed a new building, and could have avoided a hefty investment.

The first step in transforming operations is to design and develop an effective operating system: the engine of the improvement programme. But even the best technical solution won't be sustainable unless it is aligned and integrated with an appropriate management infrastructure and the right mindsets and behaviours. The next chapter sets out our approach to developing a management infrastructure capable of supporting and sustaining the new operating system.

CHAPTER 4

Management Infrastructure

- To make change stick, it's essential to put the right management infrastructure in place.

- There are five main aspects of management infrastructure to consider in a typical lean transformation.

- There is no 'one size fits all'; the nature of the management infrastructure depends on the operating system.

Operational performance improvement programmes have earned a bad reputation. They tend to fail. Many deliver temporary gains, but few succeed in sustaining the early benefits, and fewer still manage to establish a genuine culture of continuous improvement. In most cases, operational performance either slips back to its old level or stagnates within a year. The latest initiative is soon consigned to history, joining a host of previous efforts in the company archives.

Why is this? In our experience, the reason isn't usually a lack of effort or expertise in addressing technical issues. It's more likely that managers have failed to recognise how easily technical improvements can unravel. Though some changes are irreversible, such as process automation or the redesign of physical layouts, most are not. And even where lasting technical improvements are achieved and early performance gains are held, it's rare to find strong foundations for delivering continuous improvement.

One defence manufacturer launched a pilot improvement project in its machine shop, which makes large and complex parts for later assembly. Senior managers believed that the machine shop was running out of capacity and acting as a bottleneck in the manufacturing process. The primary objective of the pilot was to improve the equipment utilisation (the overall equipment effectiveness, or OEE) of a number of machines, each of which had a capital value of several million euros.

The manager in charge of the machine shop believed that raising the OEE would enable him to release substantial processing capacity and thus accommodate future business growth without major capital investment. A project team identified ways to eliminate problems and developed ideas for technical improvement, such as moving stocks of raw materials and improving loading procedures to eliminate unnecessary machine and crane operations. When implemented, these ideas quickly led to an improvement in OEE of over 50 per cent.

Within a few weeks, however, the improvements began to fall away, and after six months OEE was only about 20 per cent higher than when the initiative began. The problem lay not in the technical improvements, which had clearly worked in the initial stages, but in the area manager's inability to hold on to the gains.

Closer examination revealed that his span of responsibility was too great: he had no shift managers in his team of 160 staff, only a 24-hour, four-shift operation of team leaders who lacked the necessary management skills. Operating such a flat organisation left him feeling that he was trying to hold on to the gains single-handed. Such a structure might just have worked in a stable manufacturing process where operators performed unskilled tasks repetitively, but it was doomed to fail in a relatively unstable and complex process demanding highly skilled operators. The company decided to add a new layer of four shift managers, each leading four or five team leaders, to enable it to recapture and sustain the improvements it had achieved in the pilot.

Every company undertaking a lean programme will need to consider whether its formal management processes, organisation structure and capability-building infrastructure reinforce its new lean operating system. If the management infrastructure is not aligned properly, the operation is unlikely to achieve its performance objectives.

To see how this works, consider a company that has introduced new *kanban* arrangements for organising in-process inventory or parts stocks. Properly implemented, these arrangements will reduce stock-outs, smooth flow, simplify production planning and enable Just-in-Time delivery. But operators and production planners can only implement them correctly if other processes and structures are brought into line. Planning and scheduling will need to be revised to prevent competing production instructions being issued to upstream processes. New local performance metrics and management review processes must be introduced to provide incentives for operators to respond to the *kanban*. Training will be required, and may entail changes to skills matrices and records.

So how does a company go about aligning its management infrastructure with its operating system? In the rest of this chapter we describe the key elements in developing a lean operating environment.

We have identified five key elements of a management infrastructure designed to support a lean operation (see Figure 4.1). The relative importance of each element will depend on the operational setting.

Figure 4.1 The five elements of management infrastructure

Organisation Structure

As the defence manufacturer's experience suggests, an operating system can't perform effectively and efficiently unless the right organisation structure is there to support it. We have found that three key aspects of organisational structure determine whether it is aligned with the operating system: the size of the front-line team, the role of the team leader, and the spans of control and levels of hierarchy in the organisation.

Team Size

At Toyota, a typical production line team consists of between four and eight employees with a working team leader. At Mars/Masterfoods, a single shift production manager might oversee a team of 40 or 50 on a confectionery line, while on a chocolate line a typical team might be only 10 or 20 strong. Why do team sizes vary so much, and does it matter?

Different technical processes place different demands on the operators who work them and the managers or team leaders who oversee them. Size matters because getting it wrong can be disastrous: the technical process may become unmanageable, or management and supervisory costs may escalate. Sometimes front-line teams are structured, sized and skilled with considerable thought. More often, they evolve through custom and practice until the rationale for their structure and size has been lost and they may no longer be geared to the demands of the technical processes they operate.

So how should lean companies determine the size of their front-line teams? We have identified several criteria that we believe managers should consider when determining optimal team size (see Figure 4.2). These criteria apply to service industries and back-office processes as much as to manufacturing industries.

Criterion	Sample indicator	Size of front-line team	
		Small (<4)	Large (~50)
Process stability	% OEE	Low	High
Process criticality	Cost of an error	High	Low
Physical layout	Number of areas	Complex	Simple
Complexity of tasks	Training hours/week	High	Low
Work content	Takt time x variants	High	Low
Required pace of improvement	% improvement/month	Rapid	Gradual

Figure 4.2 Drivers of team size in operations

The more complex the work content or set of tasks to be performed, the greater the need for management intervention in the running of the operation. Conversely, the more stable the process, the fewer interventions managers need make and the wider the management spans can be, allowing larger front-line teams.

The more critical the process is in terms of the cost of any malfunction, the more time the manager or team leader will need to spend dealing with problems when they arise. In such situations, a smaller span of management reduces the risk of expensive failures.

Team Leader's Role

High-calibre managers may be able to handle wide spans of control, whereas working team leaders who spend much of their time on the job can oversee only small teams. One well-known consumer goods company is able to have large teams not just because most operators carry out simple, repetitive packing tasks, but also because it employs first-rate (and well paid) shift managers.

Countless different models exist for defining the role of the team leader or front-line manager. They vary in the way they group together process steps, organise work shifts, assign roles between teams and their managers, and so on. At one extreme is a self-managed team that runs operations autonomously by dividing up responsibilities between its members. At the other is a front-line manager who bears full responsibility for a line or shift, and combines the duties of a supervisory team leader with broader aspects of HR management such as recruitment, formal appraisal and discipline.

Between these extremes lie a multitude of other models. A working team leader might combine direct operational tasks (such as covering for absentees) with some day-to-day personnel management (such as managing overtime). A supervisory team leader, on the other hand, might spend all of his or her time managing the hour-by-hour needs of the process and the operators under his or her control, doing no operational work and holding no responsibility for annual staff appraisals or discipline.

So which model works best? Everything depends on the context. The choice depends on the nature of the management tasks demanded by the operating system, and the company's underlying approach to personnel management.

At one manufacturing company we know, self-managed teams work well because the nature of the process largely determines where operators are located and the tasks they perform, and because many of these operators have years of experience. But this model could easily fail in less established organisations where staff turnover is high, or where the shop-floor culture discourages operators from taking on management duties, or where a culture of continuous improvement hasn't yet become ingrained. We visited one manufacturer that took pride in its self-managed teams, yet a glance at the figures revealed that productivity levels hadn't improved in the past five years.

Contrast this with Toyota, where team leaders form the backbone of the production organisation. About half their time is spent covering for absentees, about 20 per cent is set aside for responding to problems highlighted by *Andon* calls, and the rest is devoted to tasks such as training or off-line quality checks. Both production roles and team sizes are clearly defined. The company works to a base level of 5.5 full-time people per team, varying it in individual cases according to the level of automation, the training requirements and the safety risk. In an area such as assembly where considerable on-the-job training is needed, for instance, teams will be smaller to give the team leader time to provide it. In highly automated areas such as the press shop, teams can be larger.

Spans of Control and Levels of Hierarchy

The criteria used in determining the size of front-line teams also apply to the design of the management hierarchy. Managers running complex departments with unstable processes or poorly trained subordinates need small spans of control. Those in charge of stable, repetitive operations with competent and well trained subordinates can cope with much bigger spans.

As for the levels of hierarchy, they should be kept to the smallest number consistent with appropriate spans of control at each management level. Where levels are few, management is physically closer to the shop floor and feedback times are shorter, improving information flow and clarity and speeding up decision making. Even in a large operation, it should rarely be necessary to have more than three levels between, say, a team leader and an operations director. In manufacturing, the roles corresponding to these levels might be shift manager, area manager or superintendent, and production or factory manager.

Although minimising the levels of hierarchy may limit opportunities for promotion and management development, it has the virtue of simplicity. It helps everyone understand their roles and enables senior managers to organise their management and communications processes effectively.

Once the organisation structure is aligned with the lean operating system, it's time to consider the second element in the management infrastructure.

Performance Management System

Enhancing employees' performance depends on motivating and developing them in line with the organisation's goals. This calls for a good understanding of the relationship between mindsets and behaviours (as we shall see in Chapter 5) as well as effective performance management processes. In our experience, the performance management system is often the weakest link in the management infrastructure that underpins the lean operating system.

One business we know took pride in its performance reporting system, which was capable of producing any report you might think of at the touch of a button. Even so, operational performance was suffering, and management realised that the system wasn't giving them the information they needed. It turned out that the metrics the system tracked weren't related to the real cost and quality drivers of the business: namely, productivity per person-hour and defect levels per item manufactured. Fortunately, the problem was fairly easy to correct, but this example does show how the mere presence of a reporting system can delude management into assuming it is in touch with performance.

One fast-food company used food scrap performance as a criterion for evaluating and rewarding store managers. Though this approach succeeded in focusing managers on an important cost driver, customers often faced a long wait for their orders. Any pre-prepared items couldn't be stored for more than 10 minutes for health and safety reasons, so the store managers cooked all meals to order to avoid waste. The company's choice of metric certainly ensured its food was fresh, but failed to meet customers' expectation that fast food should be just that.

A great performance management system in a lean operation is much more than just a colourful set of reports, or the tracking of the right metrics; it goes right to the heart of management. It calls for not only a clear system definition – the right metrics, supported by effective tracking and reporting processes, IT tools and linkages to financial and other systems – but also the right approach to managing the dynamics of performance hour by hour, shift by shift, day by day, month by month. What's more, the people who operate the processes must be able to see and understand the critical measures of performance so that they can take the right steps to make high performance an everyday reality.

Setting up a lean performance management system involves several steps: designing the system, setting targets, monitoring day-to-day activities, setting up personnel systems, setting personal objectives, and managing individual performance.

Designing the System

Before a company can start actively managing performance, it needs to establish the right formal architecture for its operating system. It should begin by articulating its top-level business goals: examples might be a cost reduction of 10 per cent, 100 per cent on-time-and-in-full deliveries, and customer rejects of 2 parts per million within the next three years. Selecting these key operational objectives is not as simple as it sounds, and companies often have too many; we worked with one company that had 21! Making trade-offs across so many objectives on a daily basis is impractical and produces unpredictable results. Instead, managers need to be presented with a concise list of indicators to help them prioritise.

The next step is to build a hierarchy of metrics throughout the organisation that link the main drivers at the lowest levels back up to the core top-level objectives. Care is needed to ensure that the lower-level metrics add up to those at the higher level, that all key metrics are covered at each level, and that each metric has a clear mathematically based definition so that the data required to calculate it is readily available or can easily be obtained through changes to data-capture mechanisms.

Once these key performance indicators (KPIs) have been defined at every level, managers must decide how they will be reported and who will be responsible for collecting and reporting them. If an IT tool is to be used, it will need to be evaluated to ensure it is fit for the purpose or capable of having its database architecture or algorithms modified. Often a new KPI definition will require changes to the manual data collection methods that feed into the IT system.

Setting Targets

This step in the process links the one-off system set-up with the dynamic performance review cycle. The top-level objectives must be carefully reconciled with the bottom-up improvement plans developed by the front-line teams and their leaders if the improvement plans are to be robust. Ambitious stretch targets should be treated with caution. They can prove an effective shot in the arm for businesses that need to make a step-change to survive and for those trying to galvanise a workforce into making bold changes; used routinely, though, they soon become demoralising. People quickly become worn down and lose heart if they are set targets they know they have little chance of attaining.

Monitoring Day-to-Day Activities

Needless to say, this must take place at every level of the organisation, though it will probably take different forms and occur at different frequencies. A team leader might well cycle around the shop floor once an hour; a chief executive, once a quarter. 'Cycle' has nothing to do with bicycles, but refers to the 'plan, do, check, act' framework popularised by W. Edwards Deming.

The first step in the cycle is the development of an improvement plan designed to meet the targets that have been set. For a team leader, the plan could be as simple as deciding to redeploy operators to make up for a production shortfall in the past hour; for a chief executive, it might be a detailed set of proposals for making major long-term improvements to the operation.

After the plan has been executed (the 'do' stage), progress is reviewed ('check'). Performance review is an area where many companies fall short. To manage it effectively, team leaders and managers must acquire the habit of questioning the gaps between actual performance and targets, and the skill of drilling down to reach the real causes of performance deficits. This is the difference between measuring and managing performance.

The final stage of the cycle involves integrating corrective actions, each with clear ownership and deadlines, into the existing improvement plans. The organisation's adherence to and constant modification of these improvement plans then becomes an aspect of performance that needs to be managed like any other.

Setting up Personnel Systems

The personnel systems needed to manage and motivate people have two main components: individual performance reviews and incentive systems.

Although many companies operate appraisal systems to review individual employees' performance on a regular basis, some businesses have no routine processes in place for front-line staff. They need to develop formal personnel reviews and support them with procedures for dealing with serious performance issues.

Incentive packages must be constructed so as to reward individual and team performance in accordance with a clear set of rules. An effective incentive system will fit with the organisation's culture and the value it places on team or individual efforts, and financial or non-monetary rewards.

Setting Personal Objectives

Personal objectives should be aligned with business objectives and defined by reference to the acronym 'SMART': specific, measurable, achievable, results-oriented and time-bound. There must be no room for misinterpretation. A personal plan should reflect an employee's commitment to strive to achieve the objectives and an employer's commitment to provide any training and guidance or development opportunities that may be necessary.

Managing Individuals' Performance

Managers need to be alert to the impact of mindsets and behaviours on performance. Once they have identified a problem, they need to be capable of handling it sensitively through feedback and coaching and, if necessary, through disciplinary procedures. As Toyota's teams demonstrate, effective production teams with a built-in performance orientation are perfectly capable of managing their own discipline. The reward system must ensure that high performance is acknowledged and rewarded appropriately. Lean companies often choose to reward the performance of a front-line team as a whole rather than focus on individual achievements.

The next element in the management infrastructure is concerned with establishing the conditions to sustain lean operations over time.

Continuous Improvement Infrastructure

A lean operation without Continuous Improvement (CI) capability won't stay lean for long. It will be unable to adapt to changing customer demands and cost and quality pressures. Little by little, hard-won performance gains will be eroded.

So how do you set about building CI capability? Although training courses may raise awareness and boost enthusiasm, they aren't enough in themselves. More often than not, enthusiasm turns to frustration when people encounter the inevitable obstacles and find themselves struggling without support.

Companies that excel at operations normally have a dedicated CI infrastructure that was set up specifically to support line management through a lean transformation. Take Valeo, a French automotive parts supplier. Continuous improvement is a key element of the Valeo Production System (VPS). New recruits spend their first week at a training school that inculcates the fundamentals of VPS. At plant level, managers are supported by a VPS facilitator who reports to a branch expert charged with maintaining consistent support across the group. An independent audit team regularly visits each plant to check progress against 20 performance indicators and ensure that improvement plans are rigorously implemented. If this sounds like a huge effort, it is. Valeo dedicates about 0.5 per cent of its workforce to the VPS infrastructure.

By studying success stories like Valeo's, we've identified three vital activities that are likely to fall outside the abilities or scope of line management and so need to be performed by a CI function:

- **Developing a consistent vision and methodology for the organisation**. Individual teams may produce their own visions of how their area should operate and maps of future-state value streams, but there is still a need for the CI function to ensure consistency of approach across a plant, and especially a multi-site organisation. Lean tools and techniques can often seem alien or inaccessible at first sight, so the CI function has an important role to play in creating standard training materials by selecting the most suitable tools and documenting them in language appropriate to the organisation.

- **Building the organisation's capability**. There is more to this than training: it also involves changing mindsets and behaviours, which in turn entails winning people's hearts and minds. A dedicated CI function can provide both classroom instruction and on-the-job coaching to model and reinforce the behaviours needed in a successful lean transformation.

- **Acting as a ring-fenced resource to support implementation**. It's when teams try to apply their new skills that they need most support. A CI function should be on hand to resolve technical issues and help tackle obstacles. It must also spread knowledge and best practices across the organisation and reach out to colleagues elsewhere who may already have found a way to overcome a particular problem. Transforming an operation also requires effective project management, and a CI function can support line managers both in overseeing the improvement programme and in structuring the work to maintain the pace of progress.

So what should a CI infrastructure look like in practice? There are three main factors to consider in design:

- **Organisation structure and size**. How many people will be needed to provide the necessary support? Which of them are best located in the plants, and which located centrally at group level? What are the reporting lines between these plant and group resources, and how does each of them link in with line management?

- **Pivotal roles and responsibilities**. Should there be internal consultants, coaches, champions, change agents or improvement engineers? Should roles be standardised and competency-based, as in the certification of green and black belt project managers for the six sigma problem solving methodology?

- **Skills and capabilities**. Do the necessary skills already exist within the organisation? If not, should consultants be used, or can people be recruited from outside or developed internally? How long will it take to acquire the necessary skills, and how can it best be done?

What kind of CI infrastructure a company needs also depends on the stage it has reached in its lean journey. There are typically three stages, which we characterise as begin, build and embed:

- **Begin**. At this stage, the primary need is to demonstrate change. Work focuses on transforming a pilot area within a single value stream. At the same time, the company must build the CI infrastructure and capability to manage the programme. While one full-time change team helps implement the future-state operating system in a pilot area, another team might work on plant-wide issues with senior managers. Both teams will need people with lean expertise to provide technical advice and guidance; in smaller companies, a newly recruited manager could perform this role. External consultants are also widely used at this stage. For a typical pilot area of 50 to 100 people, say, the team is likely to consist of one or two lean experts together with two or three change agents drawn from the pilot area or other parts of the organisation. The key skills will include designing the improvement programme, training and coaching, and developing technical knowledge.

- **Build**. Many companies' change efforts stall during this second stage because the supporting CI infrastructure is inadequate. As the emphasis shifts to managing the transformation programme, the scope widens to encompass multiple value streams. Change agents who served their apprenticeship during the first stage now become managers of a new team, training fresh change agents in their turn. After a few cycles, they may well move to a group-level team where they act as internal consultants, reducing the need for outside support. Project management becomes crucial, as does managing an effective capability-building effort. The fledgling CI function must mature into a respected advisory role and help build the infrastructure to support company-wide implementation.

- **Embed**. By the last stage, every value stream will have undergone a lean transformation; continuous incremental change becomes the norm. Only the best lean companies get this far, and even they don't make it in one go. Little extra support is now needed: just a few specialists who train new managers and support shop-floor *kaizen* improvement teams working under the direct control of operations managers. Rather than being pushed from the centre, coaching is pulled by line operators and managers who request it to help them meet targets. Solid technical knowledge and practical coaching and change management skills are the crucial capabilities for the CI function at this stage.

The skills and processes that help to build them are central to the fourth element in the management infrastructure needed to support a lean operating system.

Processes for Developing Operational Skills

Any major change effort is bound to stretch both the individuals involved and the organisation as a whole. In the process, it will bring to the surface latent skill gaps. This can be disturbing, especially for seasoned managers who suddenly discover that the skills that have served them well throughout their career are out of step with the new operating system.

A lean transformation presents particular challenges for managers who pride themselves on their firefighting skills. Time after time, organisations whose operations have become unstable grow to rely on managers who are effective firefighters. As they are promoted to key roles, firefighting becomes ingrained in the culture. But a lean transformation aims to put out these fires for good – so what becomes of the firefighters? The skills it takes to refine and manage a stable operating system are quite different from those in their repertoire.

To develop the right operational skills, the organisation needs to add two core elements to its management infrastructure: a management process that identifies and codifies the skill sets required to manage the operation, and a set of programmes (training courses, apprenticeships, academies, on-the-job-coaching and feedback) that will support the building of these skill sets and their associated administrative systems.

DEFINING THE SKILL SETS

The skills operators need to do their jobs are determined by the tasks they perform. However, ensuring that the operation has the right supply of the relevant skill sets both across the workforce and within each shift calls for careful management. One common approach is to design a robust skills matrix of 'named operator' by 'specific skill demanded by the process'. This should ideally be linked into the personnel management system so that skill requirements can be matched to the individuals available at any one time.

In a lean environment, the skills line managers need typically revolve around real-time performance management, root-cause problem solving and the ability to lead small teams in looking for ways to improve operations through coaching, personnel development and so on.

DESIGNING THE CAPABILITY-BUILDING PROGRAMMES

Programmes need to be comprehensive, relevant and tailored to particular groups, with a good mix of formal training, on-the-job development and coaching. Some organisations set up their own academy or school to build practical skills. Once it has trained employees, it gets them to apply their new skills and reviews their progress systematically. The challenge of closing any significant skill gaps must be a top priority for senior managers. Indeed, they may well find they need to learn new skills themselves to manage the new way of working.

The last element in a lean management infrastructure has to do with the delivery of functional support to front-line teams and processes.

Management of Key Functional Support Processes

Twenty or 30 years ago, most large corporations sought to gain economies of scale by centralising functions such as personnel, maintenance and planning. The result of this policy was that functions began to operate in silos, with key accountabilities separated at a very high level in the organisation. For example, senior managers from production, engineering, maintenance, quality, planning and technical services would all report directly to the operations director. In such structures, each local production unit received functional support through a variety of formal and informal processes and cross-functional teams whose effectiveness depended on the quality of personal relationships at the front line. Conflicts between functions (over whether to rework defective products, say) frequently had to be taken to top management for arbitration. Not surprisingly, most businesses have since moved away from this model.

In sharp contrast, the value-stream organisation devolves all the functional skills and accountabilities needed to manufacture a product or deliver a service to a much lower point in the organisation: the value stream. Each value-stream manager – of which there could be several for any operating unit – can therefore operate far more autonomously, which speeds up decision making and problem resolution.

The reality for most organisations today lies somewhere between these two extremes. Figure 4.3 illustrates several different ways of organising functional support. Model 1 shows the full integration of the functional activity into the front-line team; Model 4 depicts the 'functional silo' approach. The two models in between deliver functional activity to

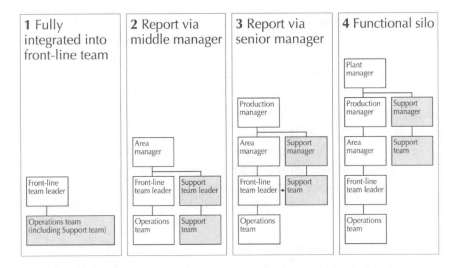

Figure 4.3 Models for organisation of support functions

the front line at progressively more senior levels in the organisational structure.

In practice, organisations create many variations on these basic models as they adopt structures that suit their particular circumstances. A manufacturer might want to divide its maintenance function into reactive and planned maintenance, for instance, with reactive maintenance fully integrated into front-line teams and planned maintenance reporting to the area or value-stream manager. In such a structure, a shift quality assurance (QA) person who reports to a senior QA manager can provide service to shift teams through service-level agreements.

So how does a lean company set about choosing the best design option? We have drawn up a set of six criteria to help managers decide when to devolve functions to value streams, when to keep them in separate silos, and when to craft a compromise between the two:

- **Frequency of interaction**. Where a front-line team interacts frequently with a function to carry out tasks or solve problems, it makes sense to integrate the functional activity into the team. If unplanned line stops are frequent, for example, it's a good idea to have reactive maintenance capability within the front-line team.

- **Urgency of need**. Where the need for functional support is likely to be urgent – because the cost of a machine standing idle is very high, say – that support should be provided either within the front-line team or through a high-quality service level agreement (SLA). One manufacturer had a reactive maintenance agreement for a piece of equipment that required specialist skills. The SLA committed central maintenance to providing a rapid response service that entailed repairing 80 per cent of failures within 15 minutes. Targets were regularly tracked, reported and reviewed by the managers involved.

- **Scarcity of skills.** If skills are in short supply, it may be best to nurture them within the function, not the front-line team. Control maintenance is often highly specialised and required across a whole operation. Its technicians need the care and attention of senior engineers to give them access to the latest developments and training as well as incentives to stay in the organisation.

- **Efficient deployment of skills.** If there isn't enough work within a single front-line team for an individual with a functional role, then that person could be deployed across multiple front-line teams, in which case a functional silo model will probably work best.

- **Access to shared facilities.** The need for access to expensive centralised equipment, systems or information is another argument for providing functional activity through a silo structure.

- **Independence from the front line.** Some functional activities, such as audit, assurance and industrial engineering, call for a degree of objectivity and independence on the provider's part and are best handled centrally in a silo model.

Where functional activity ends up being deployed directly into the front-line team, strong links – both formal and informal – need to be maintained with the central function. These help to ensure that appropriate functional controls are in place and facilitate access to central resources such as company-wide fault databases and root-cause analysis tools used in maintenance. They also enable best practices to be shared across the whole organisation.

Most lean transformations tend to focus on the more tangible support processes such as maintenance, but companies also need to make sure that other less prominent functional elements provide the right support.

Take cost management systems. If front-line managers are to take responsibility for driving continuous improvement in labour productivity, they need to know that these systems correctly track the labour hours and costs in their area so that they can measure the progress they are making. But the systems have probably evolved over time, and may not precisely meet the needs of the lean transformation. Any mismatches could easily thwart line management's efforts.

Several other functional support processes fall into this category: quality management systems, people management processes (such as resource planning, labour scheduling and attendance, holiday and sickness management systems) and IT configuration. Each must be designed to fit with the lean operating system so that it promotes efficient production rather than hindering it. Managers need to give as much thought to these issues as they do to getting the right *Takt* time if they are to achieve a stable and efficient operation that is properly supported.

Many managers will find adapting to their new way of working quite a stretch. Indeed, as we see in the next chapter, it usually requires a completely new mindset and approach to their role.

CHAPTER 5

Mindsets and Behaviours

- Mindsets and behaviours underpin (and can undermine) formal systems.

- Some generic lean mindsets and behaviours are counter-intuitive.

- Mindsets and behaviours must be matched to the needs of a particular operating system.

Even the best operating system supported by the most complementary management infrastructure won't produce the desired results unless people behave in a way that supports the operating system. The right formal systems, structures and processes are necessary to make change stick, but they aren't sufficient. In any lean transformation, individuals' actions need to change; for that to happen, people at every level of the organisation must be engaged and committed.

By mindsets and behaviours, we mean the way people think, feel and act, both individually and collectively. Human motivation is never straight-forward, and behind every action people take lie a multitude of beliefs, attitudes, aspirations and values that ultimately determine how they will respond to the challenges they face.

What makes this a minefield for managers is that while behaviours can be observed, mindsets can't. I might tell you what my attitude to something is, but can you trust what I say? Am I telling the truth? Do I even know myself all that well? The links between mindsets and behaviours aren't transparent or predictable.

One of the basic truths about behaviour is that just telling people what to do is seldom enough. Imagine how you might feel if you were told to do something without understanding how you should do it, or why. For most people, being given orders feels coercive – an affront to their autonomy. They may comply, but they'll probably feel resentful, which won't dispose them to be cooperative in future.

Though effective in a crisis – 'Mind that car!' – orders still rely on a shared understanding of the situation and a willingness to comply. Seeing the speeding car and realising that the command is in your own interests, you obey. In the same way, people are more likely to carry out an instruction if they believe it will ultimately benefit them; if they don't, or think it might harm them, they will probably ignore or resist it.

To complicate things still further, groups of people often behave in the same way for completely different reasons. Imagine that a manager embarking on an improvement effort asks his four team members to fill in a simple log sheet throughout the day to record progress and list any problems they encounter. The manager gives them clear instructions and makes sure they have the resources they need, but not one of them complies. Why?

One team member thinks the improvement effort is just another management fad that will peter out after a few weeks like all the rest. Another dislikes the manager and wants to make trouble for him. The third is worried about what the new way of working might mean for him. The fourth senses her colleagues' reluctance and goes along with them out of solidarity. Here are four different mindsets all culminating in the same behaviour.

What lessons can be drawn from this? First, you can't find out what motivates people by watching what they do; you can ask them, but that probably won't give you the answer either. Second, it's better to assume you don't know someone's motivation rather than that you do; accept that we all have our individual motivations, and try not to generalise. Third, behaviour often changes even where there is no obvious stimulus, especially in a dynamic situation like a change effort.

Believing that behavioural change can be imposed, some managers expect automatic compliance and unquestioning obedience. But why *should* subordinates fall into line if they aren't given reasons and explanations? The manager's responsibility is not to enforce total compliance, but to encourage common purpose.

In this chapter, we describe what we might call the generic lean mindset, show how it translates into a different way of behaving, and explain how a company should match new lean mindsets and behaviours to its new lean operating system. We also look at several case studies that bear out the importance of aligning mindsets and behaviour with operating system and management infrastructure to accomplish a successful change programme.

The Lean Mindset

Lean thinking starts with the customer and works back from there, defining any activity that doesn't add value for the customer as waste.[1] The goal of the lean organisation is to strive constantly to deliver value to the customer in the shortest possible time through the relentless elimination of waste, variability and inflexibility. Certain ideas are common to all lean companies, and contribute to what we might call the lean mindset. Some of them run counter to the prevailing mindset in many conventional organisations.

DON'T THINK BIG; THINK SMALL AND FLEXIBLE

One of the goals of a lean transformation is to drive down lead times to allow a company to respond quickly to its customers' changing demands. This involves designing both core processes and the organisational structure to create flow. For executives schooled in the guiding principle of scale economies – namely, using expensive equipment to process large batches in order to drive down unit cost – such an approach may seem perverse.

A lean mindset views common problems in a very different light. Think about boarding a flight. Where there is no direct gangway access, big buses are used to transport passengers in batches from the terminal building to the plane. You have to wait in the lounge for the bus to arrive, wait on the bus for the last passenger to get on and then queue on the tarmac to board the plane. The operating system is characterised by stagnation rather than flow.

Now let's consider how we might apply a lean mindset to tackle passengers' frustration. If more journeys were made with smaller buses, waiting time would be reduced. This would incur higher capital investment and a heavier salary burden, but substantially increase value to passengers through better service.

THE FRONT LINE IS WHERE THE VALUE GETS ADDED

When you go to a supermarket, you want to find good products quickly and pay for them without queuing for too long. If you can't find something, you need a friendly member of staff to show you where it is. As a customer, you don't care how many deliveries were made last night, or what training schemes the till operators have been on, or what key performance indicators the retailer tracks. For sure, the supermarket may need all these things to deliver value to you, but they don't form part of

---

1   James Womack and Daniel Jones coined the phrase 'lean thinking' in their book *Lean Thinking: Banish Waste and Create Wealth in your Corporation*, London, Simon & Schuster, 1996.

your shopping experience, or your perception of value. Obvious, perhaps – but managers often have difficulty accepting the implications. They may have to adjust their own roles and the way they allocate their time between different tasks in order to ensure that front-line operations run smoothly and value is added at the customer interface.

Everyone in the Organisation Needs to Understand How His or Her Actions Contribute to Business Goals

Consider a company that has always operated with a high level of over-time. Because of falling demand, the business no longer needs this expensive additional capacity. Employees who have become used to the extra income will need to understand the business reasons for withdrawing it before they can accept the change. The withdrawal of overtime will need to be offset by some other perceived benefit such as job security. Managers must be transparent, not only to demonstrate the need for change but also to earn trust and help align the interests of individual employees with those of the company. Such alignment forms the necessary basis for employees to develop a lean mindset and take on the extra responsibilities that a lean system demands.

The Root Causes of Problems Need to be Addressed, Not Just the Symptoms

In unstable operating systems, as we have seen, people spend most of their time reacting to problems. Over time, they become adept firefighters, their behaviour is rewarded, and firefighting becomes part of the culture. In a lean environment, by contrast, problems are not tolerated. Instability is anathema to a lean mindset. Any source of loss is pursued back to its root causes and designed out to prevent recurrence.

At Toyota, any problem is brought to light as quickly as possible so that it can be resolved there and then. Employees are obliged to stop an entire car production line if they detect a fault. The root causes must be resolved before production resumes.

A Problem is an Opportunity to Improve, Not to Blame

A regime based on punishment quickly becomes oppressive and invites rebellion and subversion. Children who are humiliated if they admit to mistakes soon learn it's safer to keep quiet and pretend nothing has happened. It's much the same in the workplace. Making an example of people who do the wrong thing doesn't work for long; employees will simply decide to keep their heads down and avoid being exposed. Worse, they are likely to hide problems and present everything in a positive light.

This makes it impossible to recognise and resolve problems as they arise. The consequence will be a culture of denial in which employees are only partly engaged in what they do and hold back from contributing to improvements.

As they relentlessly reduce the levels of waste in an organisation, lean improvement efforts invariably unearth problems. The challenge is to welcome these problems as they emerge, and then find ways to resolve them.

Lean Behaviours

New mindsets drive new behaviours. As Figure 5.1 shows, an organisation in which people have adopted lean principles and embedded them in their way of thinking will act in a different way.

Lean mindsets	Lean behaviours
Flexibility is more important than scale	Decisions are driven by long-term systems considerations
Value is added at the front line	Management is connected to the day-to-day reality of the front line
Everyone should understand how what they do fits with the business goals	Front-line staff are engaged in real improvement activities
The root causes of problems need to be addressed, not just the symptoms	Managers work to resolve systems problems
A problem is an opportunity to improve	There is an open dialogue between staff at different levels

Figure 5.1 How mindset drives behaviours

DECISIONS ARE DRIVEN BY LONG-TERM SYSTEMS CONSIDERATIONS
Most plant managers are proud of their newest and most advanced piece of equipment and like to show it off to visitors, partly because engineers are naturally interested in technology, but also because investment is often regarded as synonymous with improvement. People who make benchmarking visits to lean plants in Japan are often surprised to see that much of the equipment is relatively old. They may not notice that it is fit for purpose and well maintained.

Managers in a lean operation adopt a systems perspective that informs their priorities and investment decisions. They ask themselves such questions as: rather than investing in additional capacity, what can I do to get more out of my existing assets? What targeted investments should I make to create flow in my operation? Too many managers have an exaggerated sense of the role new technology can play in improving performance. Once they appreciate the benefits of flexibility over scale, their decisions and priorities will change.

MANAGEMENT IS CONNECTED TO THE DAY-TO-DAY REALITY OF THE FRONT LINE

It is essential to check that planned actions are working at the customer interface. In practice, this means management spending time at the front line, going out with the sales force to visit customers or working alongside operators on the assembly line. Only direct experience can provide the 'on the ground' knowledge needed to refine decision making.

At one large telecoms operator, a team was trying to improve fault repairs. It soon realised it needed to get out of the office and see what was going on in the field. As one manager put it: 'We had only ever done this from our offices before; we had never gone to see it for ourselves. Although we had databases full of numbers, we found that some of the most important things were qualitative, not quantitative. By shadowing a field technician for a day, we found the real root causes. Now we have structures and routines that oblige managers to spend time in the field periodically. The "go and see" principle has become part of our culture.'

FRONT-LINE STAFF ARE ENGAGED IN REAL IMPROVEMENT ACTIVITIES

How many employees live every day as though it were yesterday, doing the same things, experiencing the same frustrations, and getting the same results? It is precisely because they experience them day after day that people at the front line know the problems – and, more often than not, have good ideas for solving them. Lean seeks to align the motivations and untapped ideas of the workforce with the organisation's overall objectives to improve business performance over the long term. Continuous improvement can't be just a management activity.

In a lean organisation, everyone knows what he or she needs to do and how his or her individual efforts contribute to the big picture. Improvement activity runs right through the operation from top to bottom. One organisation had a slogan that said 'Everyone in this company has two jobs: to do their job and to improve their job.' Many companies claim to practise continuous improvement; the acid test is whether every front-line employee is engaged in real improvement activity.

MANAGERS WORK TO RESOLVE SYSTEMS PROBLEMS

Not only must managers work to understand the problems facing front-line employees in creating value for customers, but also they must take full responsibility for resolving these problems at the system level. When the telecoms operator investigated the way its call centre handled incoming calls, it found that only two out of a sample of nine employees followed the correct procedure by calling the customer when a particular fault was diagnosed. The shortfall in skills that this revealed was not a front-line problem capable of being resolved by employees, but a systemic issue demanding managerial action. It called for a fundamental rethink on staff training, and perhaps recruitment too. Without it, local teams would be left papering over the cracks, and the problem would surely recur. In a lean organisation, managers immediately acknowledge their responsibility to address underlying system and infrastructure deficits that prevent front-line employees creating value for customers.

THERE IS AN OPEN DIALOGUE BETWEEN STAFF AT DIFFERENT LEVELS

In organisations with a blame culture, employees say only what they think managers expect them to say for fear of reprisals. The effects are insidious. One retail store manager told us that she said nothing when new initiatives were announced, having learned from experience that raising concerns only got her labelled as obstructive. She found it more effective 'just to keep quiet and wait for it to fail'. In a healthy lean organisation, by contrast, people at different levels of the hierarchy can openly address the issues they face and say what they really think because they accept the joint ownership of problems.

Matching Mindsets and Behaviours to the Operating System

The ways of thinking and behaving we have just described are common to all lean organisations. Any organisation implementing a lean programme must go into more detail and decide precisely what kinds of mindset and behaviour it needs to promote so as to support its new operating system. It also needs to ensure that the desired ways of thinking and acting are consistently displayed by senior managers for others to observe and emulate.

Such role models set the tone for the rest of the organisation. In a company trying to cut costs, managers will probably need to forgo first-class travel and five-star hotels. Again and again, when helping businesses implement lean transformations, we have seen the way senior managers behave, both individually and as a leadership team, being reflected right across the organisation.

During a diagnostic at a large electronics manufacturer, we heard it reported that the CEO and director of engineering had jumped several quality gates for an important new contract, citing exceptional circumstances. This sent a terrible message to the troops, since these two were personally responsible for driving the implementation of a robust new process designed to address the lack of control over major engineering projects.

Consider too the case of the United Kingdom division of a heavy equipment manufacturer. The company launched a major improvement programme to restore delivery reliability and quality levels while at the same time reducing costs. The operating system and management infrastructure were redesigned and implementation began in two pilot areas.

After six weeks, progress was encouraging: throughput time was reduced and schedule adherence improved by 60 per cent. But the programme soon lost momentum. Work on central management systems progressed far too slowly, and there was little enthusiasm about deploying the new production system across the site.

The company decided to look into behavioural issues within the organisation, and soon discovered some of the underlying reasons for these problems. At management level, decisions were being made but not implemented, partly because managers avoided getting involved with the operators and supervisors on the shop floor, making joint problem solving impossible.

Worse, team members didn't trust one another. Older managers suspected younger colleagues were using the company as a stepping-stone to higher things, and weren't committed to its future. Younger managers criticised their elders as being conservative. Instead of reaching decisions openly in formal meetings, managers were seeking out private sessions with the managing director. Much the same issues surfaced on the shop floor, where production teams were failing to collaborate across shifts to resolve shared problems.

Senior management was inadvertently setting an example that everyone else followed. Middle managers worked in isolation; operators merely executed orders. The top team needed to hold up a mirror to see what they were doing and the impact it was having. Only then could they start to model the new behaviours required to make the change programme a success and resolve the conflicts within their organisation. Two qualities in particular characterise the behaviour of people in a lean organisation: discipline and cooperation.

We saw earlier how a *kanban* system can be used to introduce quick changeover times, correct signal levels and batch quantities, clear visual standards and levelled production. However, it won't work unless people are disciplined and respect the rules of the system, as Figure 5.2 indicates. Operators mustn't produce parts too early; they need to trust their colleagues and wait for signals from downstream processes; and they need to discuss problems with team leaders as soon as they arise so that they can be resolved quickly and don't threaten the stability of the system.

Cooperation is equally important, and applies both to the internal relationships within teams and departments and the way that functions work together. Getting different functions to collaborate in pursuit of a common goal can be tricky, especially if they have different cultures and conflicting objectives. Most functions are geared to optimising their own parts of the business rather than the system as a whole.

Let's look at a plant that produced electrical products. Only a few of these products were standardised; most were designed to order. The plant's design and production staff were in separate departments. In the past, the design department had optimised its own resources and skills while ignoring production needs and constraints. The result had been peaks and troughs in production, and bottlenecks that delayed deliveries to customers. Design's insularity had caused other production problems

Operating system	Management systems	Mindsets and behaviours
Quick changeover times	Maintenance of the system built into team leader's responsibilities	High level of discipline required to respect the rules
Calculation of correct signal levels and batch quantities	Inventory levels tracked as a driver to OTIF delivery performance (KPI)	Trust required to wait for the signal from downstream process
Clear visual standards for operator and packer		Discussion with team leader to address any problems or concerns
Levelled production	Reorganisation of maintenance support to line to ensure reliability	

Figure 5.2 Example of role of mindsets and behaviours

too: for instance, it often omitted to update the design blueprints that production operators used for reference.

As part of a lean transformation, the plant decided to integrate production planning and scheduling at the design stage, which meant that the designers would in future be compelled to take production constraints into account. This was not just an organisational change; it had implications for the mindsets and behaviours of both groups involved. To correct deep-seated problems, each department needed to understand how the other worked and be willing to exchange information and work together on resolving difficulties as they occurred.

We end with a case study that illustrates how a retail company introducing a new lean operating system discovered that changing mindsets and behaviours was both more important and more challenging than it had imagined.

Breaking the Vicious Cycle of Operational Problems

Our case concerns a European retailer with an extensive network of stores selling a wide product range. Before it embarked on its change programme, its stores were always full of people, but less than half of them actually bought anything. It discovered that its loyal customers tended to browse even when they didn't intend to buy, and that many people visited the stores on the off-chance of finding a bargain.

In recent years, the company had made heavy use of promotions to drive sales. One of the side effects of this strategy was that leftover stock from these promotions accumulated, exacerbating operational problems. In addition, product availability was poor: on average, only about 70 per cent of listed products were actually available on the shelves for customers to buy at any one time.

Rather than leaving gaps for missing products, the staff in charge of filling the shelves put out other goods in their place. As a result, the displays in stores sometimes bore little resemblance to the plans developed at head office. This made it difficult to assess how successful different products were. If sales data revealed that a product was selling well in a particular store, was it because it was genuinely popular, or because it had been given extra shelf space? The management of the supply chain also suffered, since the departure from centrally defined shelf-filling standards meant that product stock-level data was no longer reliable.

The operational needs were to clear surplus stock from the business, manage stock rooms efficiently and improve product availability. Tackling them would involve not just improving the management infrastructure, but also challenging some deep-seated behaviour. Before it could improve product availability, for example, head office needed to know what was missing, which meant that for the first few months, stores needed to leave gaps on their shelves. This left staff feeling uneasy. Resisting the temptation to fill the gaps called for understanding, discipline and a fundamental change in mindset and behaviour.

Analysis of the situation revealed that there had been a breakdown in the feedback loop between the head office functions that created and issued plans for the stores and the store managers responsible for delivering the plans at the front line. Head office had lost touch with the reality of what was going on in stores, while the stores saw its plans as unrealistic.

The change programme was structured in three main parts. First, fix the planning system by improving the effectiveness of head office's data-gathering system and ensuring that key business measures reflect reality. Second, employ in-store standards to improve adherence to the plan. Third, make sure that the new system becomes institutionalised as part of the company's culture.

The programme began with a thorough diagnostic to analyse issues including the true level of on-shelf availability and the reasons that products were often missing. In some cases, it turned out that products were available in the stock room but hadn't been put out on the shelf: because they had been delivered a few weeks later than planned, the space allocated for them had been given over to different products. In other cases, products were out of stock because of a malfunction in the stock control system, which failed to reorder goods that had been sold.

The next step was to develop solutions and test them in six stores selected as representative of the whole chain. The company devised a number of simple processes such as introducing coloured tags to identify shelf locations that had been filled temporarily by a replacement product. Such measures were intended to remind staff to reinstate the original product as soon as it became available.

However, the trials revealed that even easy-to-implement solutions like this were failing to stick, and problems were recurring. When the project team investigated, it discovered that area managers and head-office executives weren't spending enough time in the stores to understand the systemic issues that they themselves needed to work on. Even those who did weren't setting the right example.

Store managers continued to do what they had always done – fill the gaps in the shelves rather than leave them empty when a product was missing. Nor did the employees in the stores appreciate the rationale for the new procedures: to them, it didn't make sense to leave an empty space for a missing product when they could sell something in its place. Because they didn't understand, they had no motivation to work in a different way.

This lack of understanding was not the only obstacle. The stores' incentive scheme was based solely on sales and margin. The staff in the trial stores were asked to follow new practices that were likely to reduce sales in the short term, even though they were intended to improve availability and sales in the longer term. So the incentive measures were in direct conflict with the desired new behaviours. It's hardly surprising that the staff carried on as they always had.

Having uncovered these problems, the team took steps to make the change stick. It developed a simple page of guidelines to remind senior managers how to act during store visits to reinforce the new processes among employees. It asked them to agree the objectives for their visit at the beginning and then let the store manager take the lead, respecting the agreed structure and timings. The team also emphasised the importance of spending time with front-line staff and asking for their opinions.

Senior managers were also asked not to discuss any problems they noticed in front of the store team, unless they were particularly serious; instead, they should debrief the store manager away from the sales floor. This ensured they didn't inadvertently undermine the store manager's status as the principal role model for store staff. To reinforce this new balance of power between store managers and head office, the team set up a 'buddy' system whereby each store manager was allocated a manager from head office to listen to problems and provide coaching. This proved an effective and natural mechanism to help reconnect senior managers to the reality of the stores.

During implementation, the company quickly recognised that its sales-driven incentive scheme wasn't appropriate in the new circumstances. Instead, it introduced a weekly audit to assess how rigorously stores were following the new processes. Although its main aim was to help store managers identify areas needing extra attention, it also linked in to incentive structures by awarding a score for compliance. Paradoxically, this created a fresh set of problems as competition between stores, a way of life in retailing, threatened to override the discipline of embedding the new ways of working.

As this case illustrates all too clearly, the effort involved in achieving behavioural change is often underestimated. By making sure that mindsets and behaviours are given the same attention as operating system and management infrastructure right from the start, managers can avoid many of the pitfalls that beset change programmes.

In Part I of this book, we've explored the features of the lean landscape. In Part II, we join Arboria, a fictional manufacturer of domestic appliances, as it sets off on the lean journey.

PART II

The Lean Journey

CHAPTER 6

Deciding to Embark

- There must be a clear business need to transform operations.

- Knowing the risks and challenges that lie ahead, the leader of the business must take a conscious decision to act.

- There must be a plan for the early part of the journey.

In the next five chapters, we follow the experiences of a company called Arboria as it sets out on its journey to lean. Like most other organisations in this position, Arboria has no previous experience of lean principles and faces a range of challenges in improving its operational performance.

A Market Leader under Pressure

Arboria is a niche producer of premium domestic appliances: food processors, coffee machines, toasters and kettles. It has sales of around

450 million euros and employs about 3000 people. It has plants in Italy, Germany and the United Kingdom. It closed a fourth plant in France during the recession in the early 1990s. It has a small head office just outside Brussels, and a design and technology centre attached to the Italian plant.

In the mid-1990s, when consolidation in this sector was rife, the business was bought by a US manufacturer of household appliances seeking a foothold in Europe for its own products, as well as access to designs for smaller models to sell in the growth markets of China and India. After the takeover, the new owner left Arboria largely to its own devices. Recently, though, it has put pressure on the management team to grow the business while also increasing its return on capital employed (ROCE).

For the past six years, Arboria has been led by Bruno Fontana (see Figure 6.1), a dynamic Italian who has been with the company for more than 20 years, most of it spent in sales. He has a good track record of anticipating important changes in the industry and repositioning the business accordingly. As well as being a visionary, Bruno has a reputation for being emotional and unpredictable; he can be inspiring and intimidating in equal measure.

Over the past three years, the proportion of sales from new products has doubled in line with an objective set by Bruno, who had noticed that Arboria's products were beginning to look outdated. He promoted a promising manager to the post of head of design, with the mandate to rationalise and

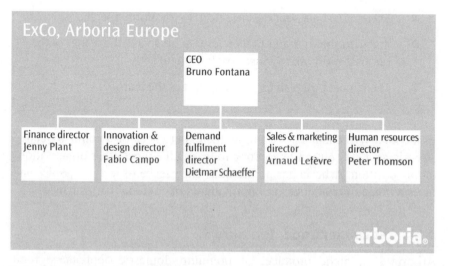

Figure 6.1 ExCo, Arboria Europe

rejuvenate the product range. Arboria launched a new range of colourful appliances, breaking with its all-white tradition, and started to develop juicing machines for health-conscious consumers.

Bruno was delighted with the product review; it had refocused the design team on customer needs. Some of the new products won design awards. The colourful appliances sold very well, introducing a new generation of customers to Arboria's products and cementing its position as the premium brand in Europe. One consequence of this success, however, was that the new products put a strain on production capacity. Arboria was unsure how it should cope with the expected growth: should it outsource part of its production or invest in new capacity?

This production quandary was compounded by concerns about pricing. In the past, consumers had been willing to pay a premium for Arboria's brand name and the reliability and design quality it embodied. But in recent years, competitors from lower-cost economies have started to pose a threat to Arboria's sales position. Escaping this price/cost squeeze and meeting its parent company's demands puts the company under pressure. Such are the matters that currently trouble Bruno.

Bruno was deep in thought as he drove to work. He was reflecting on something that Philippe de Lasset, a distributor of Arboria products in France, had said to him the previous day.

'Bruno, I can sense that a storm is brewing,' Philippe had announced over lunch. 'Though the market for your products is growing, manufacturers in the Far East and Eastern Europe are catching up with good products at good prices. Your brand might be strong now, but it won't be enough to protect you this time.'

Normally Philippe's ominous predictions didn't worry Bruno, but this time he found them unsettling. In a sense, Philippe had told him nothing new: of course cheaper imports posed a threat. What troubled him was the implication that the quality gap was closing faster than he had expected.

As a retailer, Philippe knew his customers well. He'd noticed that the buying patterns of conservative French consumers had shifted away from traditional brands towards cheaper products. His customers trusted Philippe's company not to sell rubbish, and were increasingly willing to try untested brands. One telling sign was that Arboria products weren't featuring in wedding present lists as often as they did five years ago.

Bruno pulled into his reserved space in the office car park. He'd hardly been aware of his journey; having taken this route so many times that it was entirely routine. He made the most of the half hour, using it to gather his thoughts for the day ahead. On the way home, he would reflect on the day's events, sifting them for nuggets of information or unresolved questions.

He turned off the ignition and brooded over the challenges he faced. For Arboria to take on the competitive threat, everyone in the organisation would have to engage and participate. People would have to change the whole way they worked and thought about the business. To energise them all would be a huge test of leadership, both for him and for his managers. The prospect was as daunting as it was exciting.

Weighing up the Options

Although Bruno can see he has to take drastic action, he doesn't yet know what form it might take. He is already at the crossroads where many organisations go wrong.

All too often, a lean transformation is seen as a technical project that can be delegated to operational people. Such a view betrays a deep misunderstanding of the scale and nature of the challenge. A lean transformation requires the operating processes to be redesigned from the customer's point of view, so it always has cross-functional implications that transcend operations and lead to business-wide changes in both formal processes and attitudes and behaviour.

Change on such a scale will soon grind to a halt if it doesn't have the support of the CEO and senior managers. Hands-on leadership is imperative if the organisation is to take tough decisions and navigate through the upheavals of the early days.

Bruno has recognised the need to shift the organisation into a different gear. The year-on-year incremental improvements that Arboria has relied on in the past won't be enough this time. The company needs a step-change not just to deliver its business objectives, but also to boost its energy and create a sense of urgency.

How can Bruno tell if lean is the answer to his problems? Lean makes big demands on a leader's time, and represents a long-term undertaking. If Arboria faced a pressing need to stem losses to stave off bankruptcy, a rigorous cost-cutting programme would be a better solution, just as a patient with gangrene is in need of amputation, not physiotherapy.

Bruno is acutely aware that he and his whole team will need to be fully committed to whatever course of action they decide to take, so he immediately begins to consult his senior managers and most trusted advisers.

Over the next few weeks, Bruno shared his view that Arboria had to act quickly to improve its cost position. He decided to discuss the issue formally with his team by booking half an hour on the agenda of the monthly executive committee meeting, or ExCo, as it is known at Arboria.

As Bruno expected, the meeting exposed divergent views. Jenny Plant, the finance director, argued that the only way to fix Arboria's cost base was to outsource commodity manufacturing to cheaper locations while retaining the assembly of higher-value products, at least for the moment. 'If you can't beat them, join them', she said.

Dietmar Schaeffer, the demand fulfilment director, had reservations. He'd previously been manager of the German plant, which had outsourced the manufacture of metal pressings to a supplier in the Czech Republic. Although unit costs had improved, deliveries had been unreliable and quality suffered. Dietmar thought these problems could eventually be overcome, but he argued that outsourcing could simply mean exchanging one set of problems for another. He also pointed out that Arboria lacked expertise in selecting and managing suppliers. If the company was going down this road, it shouldn't set out before it understood all the risks.

Arnaud Lefèvre, the sales and marketing director, was inclined to agree. He said that since distributors held most of the market power, there was no room for failure. Arboria was already struggling to keep up with their ever-changing requirements, and a few had recently cited its 'on time in full' performance as cause for concern.

As Arnaud saw it, lengthening the supply chain would only make matters worse. 'Our customers don't care how we organise ourselves. They just want the right products to pop out of the end of the pipe at the right time. If we make the pipe longer by outsourcing to Poland, say, we increase the risk of getting it wrong. On the other hand, if we can get our house in order on costs, we can turn it to our advantage.'

Bruno saw that the team lacked the experience and facts they needed to make a sound decision. He cut short the debate and asked Dietmar to organise a visit to a company that had faced and resolved a similar dilemma. He hoped this would give them a clearer picture of what might be involved.

Learning from Others' Experience

This first discussion of the options for change reveals a plurality of views within ExCo. As finance director, Jenny Plant takes a pragmatic line, suggesting that Arboria shouldn't be manufacturing at all unless it makes sense financially. Her logic may seem compelling, but the decision isn't as simple as it might appear.

For Jenny, the issue is how the cost of making a product in-house compares with the cost of subcontracting it. The danger with this approach, as Arnaud points out, is that it fails to take account of lead times, a factor that customers regard as important, and so can create a whole new set of problems. It also raises questions about the performance culture of the organisation, as outsourcing can be a way to avoid facing the need to improve performance internally.

Such differences of opinion can be helpful at this early stage, but a lack of alignment within the senior team is a common cause of problems later in the change journey. If discussions aren't given enough time, decisions will suffer. Building consensus can be a slow process: not everyone is willing to be forthright, and opinions sometimes need coaxing out. Rushing the debate can leave important views unvoiced and mean that discussions are reopened again later outside the meeting. In the end, it's better to give a discussion the space it deserves.

Before they can decide which path to follow, Bruno and the team need to gain a reasonable understanding of what an operational transformation involves in terms of capabilities and resources. The last thing they want is to commit themselves to a journey they will be unable to complete.

A few weeks later, the ExCo team set off to visit ATC in Rouen, a manufacturer of plastic components for the car industry. Dietmar knew Luc Bezier, the production manager, who had agreed to host a half-day visit to share his experiences of implementing lean. Unfortunately, an urgent request for figures from Arboria's US parent meant that Jenny had to pull out at the last minute.

From the moment they arrived, the team were impressed by the sense of order at the plant. While they signed themselves in, the security guard explained the site's safety procedures. As they walked across to the main building, Bruno, who enjoyed teasing Dietmar, pointed out that you could tell you weren't at Arboria: there weren't any piles of broken pallets in the loading bay.

The visit began as most do: they were ushered into a training room and given plastic cups of bad coffee. But things improved from then on. Instead of subjecting them to a long presentation, Luc handed them over to a team leader called Jerome Chevalier.

Jerome gave a candid account of the plant's chequered history, including a period when it had been troubled by strikes. He went on to talk about the introduction of lean manufacturing and the difference it had made both in the business results and on the shop floor. He used photographs to illustrate the practical improvements that production operators had introduced, and answered questions from the ExCo team as he went along. They all agreed that the results looked impressive.

The group then made their way to the shop floor. Along with the familiar smell of injection-moulded plastic, the thing that immediately struck them was the same sense of order they had met when they arrived. From the clear labelling of machines to the information boards in the meeting room, everything seemed remarkably well organised. As they walked from the injection-moulding area towards assembly, they passed boxes of plastic components stored in lines. At the loading bay, finished products were being forklifted onto a truck for delivery to a nearby car assembly plant.

Jerome called the young man who was loading the pallets and asked him to explain how he worked. The operator showed them his pick list, which stated how many of each part were required. He explained how the floor was marked with fixed locations so that he always knew where to go for each product. 'There's not much to it really. It's all pretty simple', he said, shrugging his shoulders.

Jerome led the team back into the main assembly area. They were surprised to see that the lines looked much more cramped than at Arboria. They stopped next to a production cell that had an LED display comparing the actual number of components made up to that point with the production target. Jerome explained how targets were calculated according to *Takt* time, and told them that as team leader he sometimes stepped into a flagging production cell to get it back on track.[1]

As the team watched, they could see that all the operators knew exactly what they were doing; there was a rhythm and pattern to their work. Parts didn't sit around for long; they were always being worked on or moved to the next stage. Dietmar noticed that unlike Arboria's assembly areas, which were piled high with components, there were very few parts to be seen here.

Heading back towards the mould shop, the team passed the boxes of components again. Jerome called to a woman who came over to join them. She explained that she collected parts for the assembly lines once an hour to ensure that the rhythm of assembly wasn't disrupted. She took

---

1   *Takt* time is defined as the available production time divided by customer demand; for more detail, see Chapter 3, page 30.

the coloured *kanban* cards off the boxes she had collected and put them into pigeonholes in the middle of the factory floor. At the end of each shift, the team leader from injection moulding collected all the *kanban* cards, which were then used to determine the sequence of production for the next shift.

'So you don't have any kind of central production scheduling?' Dietmar asked Jerome, partly for the benefit of his ExCo colleagues.

'No.' Jerome thought for a moment. 'Well, that's not quite true. We use it for planning raw materials and loading finished products and so on, but for the day-to-day running of production – no, we don't.'

'And does that work? Don't you ever run out of parts? What if cards go missing?' Bruno asked.

Jerome laughed. 'Actually, it works very well. I know it seems too simple, but things work better now than when we had complicated systems telling us what to do. Of course, we had difficulties at the start; I guess you always do. But once people got the hang of the new system and the discipline it takes, we got over them. Now people know that it makes their lives easier, they make it work. In fact, we're all pretty proud of the productivity gains we've achieved.'

Dietmar caught Bruno's eye. He knew what he was thinking. Scheduling was a headache at their own plants. He'd want to know why they weren't already doing things this way.

They walked on and stopped by a machine that was being changed over from one product to another. In the midst of all the activity, everyone once again seemed to know exactly what they were doing. When two people were needed to position the new mould tool in the machine, they were both there. At other times, the operators worked separately. The whole changeover process took about 20 minutes.

'This used to take anything up to four hours', explained Jerome. 'Every operator and technician had their own way of working, so nobody knew how long a changeover would take. Planning was a nightmare.'

Jerome walked over to the workstation by the machine. Tools hung on a shadow board over a small desk. On it was the shift log sheet and a few other documents. He picked up a set of laminated sheets featuring instructions and photos.

'We analysed a few changeovers with the operators and then drew up a standard process to follow. We also track how long changeovers take these days.' He showed them a chart. 'If you'd said three years ago that we could change a tool over in 15 minutes, people would've laughed. Now that they have done it for themselves they know real progress is possible; their attitudes have changed completely.'

Time had run out, so the team moved back to the training room for a final debrief. They were thoughtful as they removed their white coats. As a rule, they didn't spend much time in manufacturing plants – not even their own. Bruno was surprised how interesting the visit had been. It wasn't so much the processes, which weren't all that different from Arboria's, but the people. They seemed engaged in their work and knew exactly what they were doing.

After the team had asked a few more questions, Luc Bezier summed up. He talked about ATC's experiences over the past few years and put up a list of the key lessons they had learned (see Figure 6.2).

Bruno rose to his feet. 'I'd like to say a very big thank you to you and everyone we met today for this visit. We've been able to see for ourselves how a system like this works. I've found it extremely interesting and rewarding, and it's whetted my appetite to learn more. So, my sincere thanks on behalf of us all.'

As he sat down, he added, 'I have one last question. If you put yourself in our shoes and think back to the beginning of your own journey, what would you advise us?'

Luc Bezier thought for a few moments. 'I would say it's your job to lead the change. Of course, you must get help from people who know lean manufacturing. They are guides who can use their experience to help you decide which path to follow. They know which shortcuts are safe and which might be dangerous; you can't always tell. But they mustn't act as leaders – that's your job.

●*ATC*

Six important lessons

- **Lean starts at the top**
- **Set ambitious targets**
- **Early victories are important**
- **Listen to your people**
- **Get expert help**
- **It takes time!**

Figure 6.2 Important lessons

'I've seen far too many initiatives fail. If I had to put my finger on why ours succeeded, I think it had a lot to do with the commitment of our senior managers. Everyone in the plant noticed the difference. They knew they would see management at the beginning, making speeches and launching the ship, but they expected them to disappear soon after. When they didn't, it sent a signal to everyone. If any one thing made a difference, that was it.'

He smiled, aware he'd thrown down the gauntlet to Bruno and his team.

Making Plans to Get Started

The visit to ATC testifies to the profound impact that seeing a lean system at work can have. Not only has ExCo seen what a difference lean makes to day-to-day operations, but also it now has a benchmark for its own plants. Bruno can ask himself what it would take to make Arboria's factories like ATC's. He has seen enough to know that the answer isn't simple, but involves integrating 'hard' factors (such as systems, structures and processes) with 'soft' factors (such as culture, mindsets and behaviours). He and his team have also discovered that lean has real meaning for the people in the plant. They have built a lean system that works; they run it and they own it.

What's more, the visit was an experience that ExCo shared. The way they interacted at the plant shaped their understanding of what was happening there. With luck, this common viewpoint will help them work out a vision for Arboria's future that they can all embrace.

Such visits also have the benefit of putting managers back in touch with the realities of production. Although senior executives constantly take decisions that affect operations, few spend much time at the front line. Perhaps they don't feel comfortable, or don't see the need. But experience has taught us that forging a strong link between decision makers and the front line is vital to a successful lean transformation. Without it, chances are that feedback and learning will be limited, and decisions won't be fully implemented or produce the expected benefits. Nothing is quite like seeing for yourself.

Some organisations openly acknowledge the need to stay in touch with the shop floor. When chairman Allan Leighton hired a new chief executive to lead the transformation of Britain's Royal Mail in early 2003, he insisted that the new recruit spent his first two weeks delivering letters. Such experiences can yield invaluable insights into day-to-day operations.

Bruno had already sensed that Arboria's leadership team would need to play a pivotal role in the transformation process; Luc Bezier's warnings about not delegating the leadership only served to confirm this.

Impressed by what they had seen at ATC, the team had agreed to proceed with a lean approach in principle, provided they could identify enough potential within their plants to meet their business needs. Bruno had called Dietmar in to share ideas.

'What do you think?' he asked. 'Do we have the capability in the organisation to carry this out?'

'I don't think so, not at the moment,' said Dietmar with characteristic candour.

'So where does that leave us? Should we recruit?'

'First we need to decide where we want to start.'

'Go on.'

'I was thinking that it probably make sense to use the Bolton plant as a pilot. Although it's our worst performing site, it has a strategic role because of the size of the UK market for toasters and kettles. If lean works in Bolton, we'll see big benefits and we'll know it can work in our other plants. And if it doesn't – well, we won't be any worse off than we are now.'

'I agree,' said Bruno. 'So how do we start?'

'We need to recruit someone with substantial experience in lean to lead the effort, and we need to put together a strong change team in Bolton.' Dietmar thought for a moment. 'We should also think about how we will transfer the approach to the other plants. Maybe we should get some external support or transfer one or two people from our other plants.'

Bruno brought the conversation to a close. 'One thing at a time, Dietmar. Let's focus on Bolton first and worry about the other plants later. Why don't you start the search for a suitable candidate to take on the project and then we'll work together on developing business plans and targets.'

Over the next few weeks, the ExCo team devoted as much time as they could to working out exactly what they wanted to achieve through the operations improvement project. With marketing colleagues, they explored how customer requirements were likely to evolve in years to come, and what Arboria would have to do to maintain its market leadership. They also started to consider how they might integrate the early phases of the lean transformation with their investment plans for new products.

Meanwhile, Dietmar hired recruitment agencies to help him identify a suitable candidate for the post of lean implementation manager. Together with the Bolton plant manager, John Wexford, he interviewed a shortlist. One of the candidates, Philip Hargreaves, stood out as having the right blend of energy and experience to get the job done. A few days later, Philip flew out to Brussels to meet Bruno, and was offered the post that evening.

Bruno felt that the journey was beginning to fall into place. They had a rough idea of the route, and the makings of a crew. They were ready to set off.

Chapter 7

Exploring the Opportunity

- In assessing improvement potential, organisations need to consider all three aspects of lean: operating system, management infrastructure and mindsets and behaviours.
- The customer perspective of value must be used to identify waste.
- To develop a real sense of urgency, managers must experience problems first hand.

Arboria's management team have decided on lean as the best approach to address their business needs. Next, they must assess the current situation and identify the potential for improvement. It's crucial for them to get first-hand experience of operating problems: personal involvement not only provides a deeper understanding of the situation, but is often emotive too, provoking a powerful commitment to the challenges the company faces. It will help them build the energy and commitment to see change through, and set a precedent for their involvement in the rest of the transformation programme.

In assessing the current situation, the team should seek to identify and quantify all sources of loss within the operating system. It must also explore possible shortfalls in the management infrastructure and consider the changes in mindsets and behaviours that will be needed to sustain a lean system. This diagnostic phase is usually fairly short, perhaps just a few weeks, and sets the agenda for the early stages of implementation.

By now the Arboria ExCo team have been thinking about the implications of a lean transformation for several months, but they haven't yet made any formal announcement at the plants. Effective communication is a prerequisite to successful change, helping to shape the mindsets and behaviours of everyone involved, but it must be a two-way dialogue, not a one-way broadcast. Since this is the stage when expectations and roles begin to take shape, it's vital to involve all the key stakeholders in the right way.

Those who shape opinion through the status of their role or through their informal influence over peers must be identified early on and given meaningful roles in the transformation. This helps ensure that the corporate grapevine works with, not against, the improvement effort. Obvious though it may seem, this step is often overlooked or mishandled. Perhaps the key stakeholders aren't in the most senior roles, or don't look like change agents. Some of them may not be entirely sympathetic to the programme. It may seem easier to leave them out, but if they carry a lot of influence this may prove a risky strategy and can even lead to the programme's failure.

Dave Smith is the production manager at Arboria's Bolton plant, but his influence extends far beyond his role (see Figure 7.1). Like many middle managers, he is a survivor. He has found his natural level within the organisation and is effective in his role. Over the years, he has seen many improvement initiatives come and go. From what he's heard, it sounds like there's another one on the way.

The coffee machine wasn't working again. This was far from unusual, but it was something Dave could do without. A few years back, some bright spark had decided to contract out refreshments to cut costs. Dave didn't dispute that there were sound economic reasons for outsourcing non-core activities, but he did wonder how a factory that made kettles could decide they were non-core.

In the past few years, Arboria had won plaudits for adapting its product range to new needs and tastes. But as Dave never tired of telling his

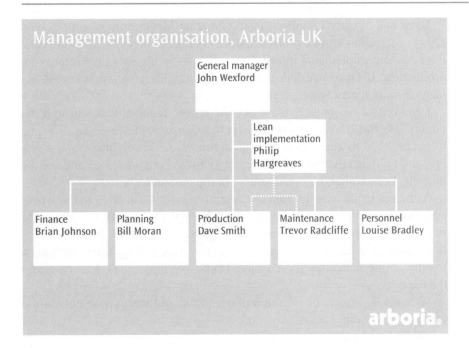

Figure 7.1 Management organisation, Arboria UK

colleagues in engineering, marketing and finance, coffee machines and kettles didn't assemble themselves. However potent the brand and stylish the design, someone still had to make the things.

Decades ago when the Bolton factory opened, Lancashire and Yorkshire had been renowned for the skills of their manufacturing base, and exported their products all over the world. Today the flow ran the other way, as the strong pound and lower labour costs in the Far East and eastern Europe forced home-grown industries to fight for survival. It was a battle that many companies had already lost. With each passing year, people wondered how much longer they could go on cutting costs and fighting a rising tide.

When Dave first joined Arboria, he couldn't help noticing that there were all kinds of opportunities to improve operations that would benefit not just the company but the employees on the shop floor too. But all his good intentions came to nothing: there was always something more urgent to deal with, another rush job to finish. He reckoned that as he was accountable for managing the day-to-day running of the factory, it was no good worrying about not having the time to improve the overall state of production.

Dave had already found out from Christine McGuire in planning, who always seemed to know exactly what was going on, that Philip Hargreaves, the new lean implementation manager, had some big ideas for improving production. If Dave had learned anything over the years, it was that big ideas usually meant trouble.

Deprived of his coffee, Dave set off on his regular walk through the factory. He did it every morning, shortly after arriving at seven. For one thing, he liked to know what was going on before his eight o'clock meeting, and he'd discovered that the best way to find out was to go and see for himself. For another, he could smoke in the despatch area.

As he made his way through the assembly lines, he chatted to the workers, mostly middle-aged women who'd been with Arboria for years. He was good with people and knew how to get the best out of them.

He looked at the empty space on the floor where the plastic mouldings for the coffee machines should have been. 'No mouldings, Fi?' he asked the team leader.

'What does it look like?' she replied. 'Same old story; problems in the mould shop again.'

'What problems?'

'How would I know? I've got enough to cope with out here without having to nanny that lot as well.'

The mouldings for the coffee machine body were always running out; that's why a buffer stock had to be set up by the assembly line. Various working teams had been asked to address the issue, but never got anywhere. The mould shop blamed poor raw materials or late changes to schedules. Purchasing accused production of using the wrong machine settings. Dave didn't care whom was at fault. All he wanted was mouldings so that he could make coffee machines and get them out of the door before he went home at the end of the day.

Although he needed a smoke, Dave decided to take a quick look at the mould shop to see what was going on. He made a detour to the planning manager's office to check how many units had been made the previous day. He found the shift handover sheet under a mug of cold coffee on Bill Moran's desk. Bill had refused to entrust an important task like making coffee to a machine, and kept a kettle in his office. Dave moved the mug and saw that after a good morning, production had failed to meet the shift target at the end of the day. He presumed the reason was a shortage of mouldings, although the handover sheet didn't say so.

He trudged off again, deep in thought. It was his walk that had earned him his nickname: 'Donkey Dave'. Unflappable and dependable, he was a reassuring presence on the shop floor.

As he entered the injection moulding shop, Dave frowned to see the machine that produced the coffee machine mouldings standing idle. There was no mould in the machine, and nobody around. Sometimes the machines looked as though they were undergoing surgery: guards off, insides spilling out onto the floor, tools everywhere. Not this time, thankfully: the machine looked OK, so it was probably just a tool changeover.

Dave spotted the mould for the coffee machine body resting on a nearby pallet. It was clean and felt cold to the touch, which told him it was ready to go in. At that moment, Guy Lanbridge, the shift supervisor in the mould shop, clapped a hand on Dave's shoulder, leaving an oily handprint on his white coat.

'Checking up on us, Dave?'

'Not you, my mouldings. What the hell's going on, Guy? We haven't received any since yesterday evening.'

'Same as ever. The schedule had us down to run toaster mouldings on the morning shift, and then change over to coffee machines. We were just setting up when planning came down in a blind panic and told us to switch to another product and change the colour. Now we haven't got any coffee machine mouldings. It's chaos.'

'Things aren't getting any better,' Dave agreed. 'Maybe Philip Hargreaves has some bright ideas up his sleeve.'

'We can only hope so. Something's got to change, that's for sure.'

'So when will this be up and running?' asked Dave, tapping the mould tool.

'Could be an hour, could be more; depends who I can get to work on it.'

'So when can I tell Fiona she'll be able to build coffee machines?'

'I reckon we'll be making the first good parts by ten o'clock. Provided we can find someone to check them, you should get your parts after that.'

'OK. I'll let them know on the line and see how I can keep them busy till then.'

Dave made his way back to the production area and passed the news on to Fiona. He suggested she start to preassemble the electrical components into the coffee machine base units. It was now nearly eight o'clock, so there wasn't time for a smoke. No coffee, no cigarette; it was going to be one of those days.

Troubleshooting the Three Aspects of Operations

Even on this short walk through the production area, Dave encounters classic sources of loss in all three aspects of Arboria's operations:

the operating system, management infrastructure and mindsets and behaviours.

The manufacturing process is organised around process villages: all the moulding machines are grouped together in the mould shop, which is physically separate from the assembly line. Because the flow between them is erratic, mouldings are stockpiled by the assembly line so that production can keep going even if the mould shop fails to deliver parts. But this expedient addresses the symptom rather than the cause of the problem. By increasing inventory costs, taking up space and prolonging lead time, it adds a source of loss to the value stream.

What's more, the haphazard stock of parts is neither owned nor controlled by the upstream process in terms of quantity, location or method of replenishment. The only real solution to this problem is to address the root causes: late changes to the schedule and excessive changeover times on the mould machine.

This problem in the operating system is compounded because an essential part of the supporting management infrastructure is missing: namely, an effective performance management system. To find out basic production data, Dave has to leave the shop floor and rummage around an office for a piece of paper. In addition, the problems with scheduling emphasise the lack of communication between departments.

The third factor in the equation is people's mindsets and behaviours. Fiona's lack of interest in the reason for the shortage of mouldings and Dave's failure to challenge her show that nobody is taking responsibility for fixing the problem. Guy may be right to blame changes to the schedule for the delay in supplying mouldings, but the time it takes to change over the mould tool is very much within his control. Guy is still immersed in day-to-day firefighting and is not stepping up to his role as team leader.

Philip Hargreaves has noticed some of these problems in his first few weeks at the factory. Since joining Arboria, he has been getting the lie of the land, meeting people at all levels and reviewing management information to understand what works and what doesn't. He's come to the conclusion that Arboria, like many mature businesses, resembles a house that's been extended over the years. The structure is a muddle, the roof leaks and the walls are cracked, but the inhabitants have grown used to the imperfections. Arboria's people work hard to get the job done, but they feel they achieve what they do not because of the system, but in spite of it.

On a personal level, Philip is excited by the challenge of mobilising the workforce to grow Arboria's market share in Europe. He thinks the strategy of bringing attractive products to market more quickly than competitors, and at sharper prices, is sound and achievable. He's also hoping that further career opportunities could arise through the US parent company and its possible expansion in Asia. But he's uneasy about Arboria's history of failed attempts to fix operations. If it has never managed to make change stick, people are going to be cynical about a new guy arriving with yet another initiative.

He's also thinking about the team he needs for the assessment. He wants Dave Smith to lead day-to-day activities under his direction; this would give him the chance to build a relationship and to coach Dave in lean principles and techniques. And Dave's undoubted influence on the shop floor would lend Philip credibility – something he badly needs as an outsider parachuted into the job by head office. Philip also intends to include Guy Lanbridge and Fiona Richardson, the team leaders from the mould shop and the assembly area, along with one or two production engineers and someone from production planning.

Philip wants all the members of the plant management team to spend one day a week on the lean implementation so that they can provide leadership and gain insights into the issues. He is convinced that if the plant manager, factory accountant, planning manager, maintenance manager and personnel manager all spend time on the shop floor making observations and conducting analyses, their eyes will be opened to the plant's hidden potential. But before he can start he needs to get agreement to take Dave, Guy and Fiona away from their regular work for a few weeks to complete the initial analysis or diagnostic.

Planning the Assessment

The initial assessment of Arboria's operations is of great importance in moving forward on the journey. The diagnostic is not only crucial in determining the root causes of the current problems and the blueprint for their resolution, but serves a very vital role in energising and engaging the team in the lean transformation.

Setting the Objectives

Philip has drawn up a plan for making an end-to-end assessment of the operating system. His difficulty is that the business need isn't yet well defined. What kind of cost improvement is Arboria looking for: a 5 per cent reduction in cost of goods sold, or a 20 per cent increase in labour productivity? Then again, at least costs are easy to quantify; flexibility is much less straightforward. Manufacturing lead times and delivery performance against customer requirements can be used as rough proxies, but they aren't the whole story.

The business problem must be defined in precise and concrete terms so that the organisation knows where it is heading and how to get there. This means doing what's necessary to fulfil the business need while expending as few resources as possible and avoiding the temptation to set excessively high aspirations. Achieving a consistent two-week lead time might give Arboria a competitive advantage; reducing the lead time further, to one week, might confer no additional benefit.

Defining the Approach

In setting out to evaluate the improvement potential, Philip must answer two questions. How much can the organisation improve when pushing performance to the limit? Will this be sufficient to address the business problem?

A valuable tool that can be used to answer these questions is Material and Information Flow Analysis (MIFA), or value-stream mapping. It involves mapping the flows within the operating system in order to identify the sources of loss – waste, variability and inflexibility – that block these flows and cause operational problems. Using MIFA enables a team to step back from the detail and understand the causes of underperformance at the system level.

In order to quantify the extent of the losses and the potential scale of improvement, other more detailed analyses will need to be completed, including inventory levels, equipment utilisation and machine fault data, waiting times, process times, activity sampling, manning levels, shift patterns, batch sizes, variations in process parameters, defect rates and delivery performance. Imagine that a detailed analysis of maintenance technicians' activities revealed that they were spending only 60 per cent of their time on repairs. The remaining time was spent on completing paperwork, waiting for jobs and performing other activities that didn't add value. If some of this administrative burden could be lifted, the freed-up time could be devoted to more productive activities.

A tool known as a value tree can be useful in such situations (see Figure 7.2). A value tree is essentially a logic tree that links various operational performance indicators (such as machine utilisation, inventory level and indirect labour costs) to a high-level business measure (such as return on sales or return on capital employed). It focuses decisions on the key levers for improvement and helps ensure that the strategy for improving operations is

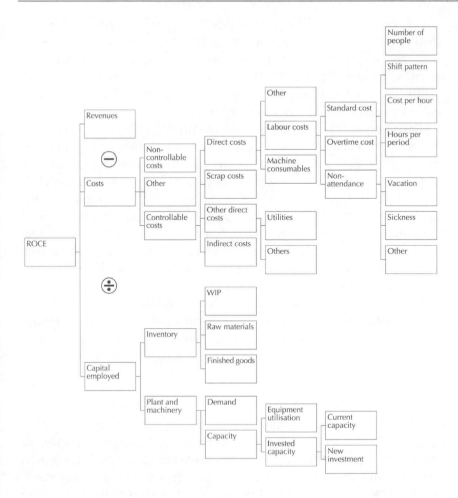

Figure 7.2 Example of a value tree

linked to overall business performance. Without this link, lean transformations can easily become fragmented and tools-based instead of integrated and results-driven.

Agreeing the Scope

Most of the analyses Philip proposes to carry out are concerned with exploring the effectiveness of Arboria's operating system. But he also needs to check that the management infrastructure supports it effectively. We've already seen that important performance data is left lying hidden under a coffee mug, and noticed signs of a lack of accountability.

A proper analysis of the performance management system will reveal whether people are focusing on the right things and what happens if performance targets are missed. If there are no real consequences, the incentive to improve will be lacking. An operating system may have well-planned material and information flows but still suffer from waste if there is no accountability for achieving results.

Motivation is central to understanding current performance levels and improvement potential. It can be explored through observation and informal one-on-one conversations as well as via formal interviews or surveys. Interviews can shed light on whether people recognise the business challenges, how difficult it will be to motivate them to change, and what the main obstacles are likely to be, such as past experiences that have inured line managers against change efforts. Similarly, a survey may reveal that middle managers don't feel senior executives trust them or consult them on important decisions. Raising awareness of such issues at this early stage can prove vital to a programme's success.

The scope of the assessment needs to be well defined. Philip has decided to look at one product family from raw materials to finished goods. He has chosen coffee machines since they are representative of the overall business and account for a substantial proportion of the total turnover at the site.

Picking the Team

Bringing together people from different functions and levels can in itself prove an effective first step to resolving problems. Managers must lead or take an active part in the evaluation of improvement potential. It's important to include 'battle-hardened' middle managers as well as 'rising stars'. Discussing issues with front-line personnel and contributing to the performance analysis will give them valuable first-hand understanding of the nature of any operating difficulties.

'Yes?' John Wexford, the general manager of Arboria UK, barked in response to the knock at the door. Philip went in. 'Oh, hi, Phil. What can I do for you?' John stood up and put out his hand.

No one else called Philip 'Phil', but John had done so from the outset, and Philip hadn't managed to stop him.

'Well, as we agreed last week I've drafted a plan for the site assessment, and I just wanted to validate it with you before we get started,' Philip said.

'Fine, let's have a look then.'

Philip passed him the page and started to explain (see Figure 7.3). 'I thought it would make sense to focus on the MIFA for the first week and then . . .'

Diagnostic plan - Coffee makers

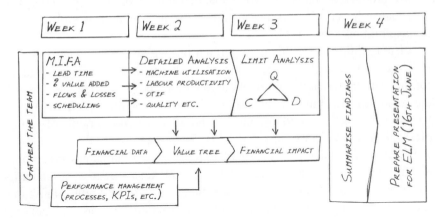

Figure 7.3 Philip's draft work plan

'The *what*?' John interrupted.

'MIFA – it stands for Material and Information Flow Analysis. It's a great way to understand the process from beginning to end and see where the problems are.'

'We've already got a pretty good idea of where the problems are, Phil. What we need is solutions.'

'Right. And this will help us find them, but it's important that the key people have a shared understanding of the main issues and root causes to start with.'

John scanned the page. 'This looks fine. I don't understand it, mind you, but I'm sure you know what you're doing. Just one thing: am I right in thinking you'll be presenting the findings to Bruno at the European Leadership Meeting on 16 June?'

'That's the plan.'

'Well, I'd like to have a good look at it before then. As I'll be away for a few days before the meeting, I'd like you to finish it in the next three weeks. Then we can set aside half a day to review it as a team. Is that OK?'

'It's not ideal,' Philip admitted. 'But I'm sure we can rejig the plan if we have to.'

'We do. Well, if that's it . . .'

'Just one more thing: the make-up of the team. I'd like Dave to lead the assessment. We'd obviously work together.'

'Donkey Dave?'

'That's right.'

'My production manager?' John sounded surprised.

'I realise he's critical to the operation, but that's why it would be great to have him take the lead.'

'Listen, Phil, I know this is important, but we've got a business to run. I've already had Bruno Fontana on my back because of the delivery figures for the last quarter, and I'm not about to risk a repeat. You can have one of the team leaders, but I'm not taking Dave out of his job. Take Fiona Richardson – she's a good organiser – and we'll get you a couple of young production engineers to support it. They'll learn a lot from this.'

Philip walked back to his office feeling uneasy. John hadn't given him his full attention, and he seemed to see the lean effort as something commissioned by Bruno, rather than something he owned himself. With a foot in both camps, Philip was in a difficult position.

Ensuring Management Ownership

Philip's conversation with John shows how difficult it can be to reconcile an improvement effort with the existing workload of running a business. It also highlights the importance of formally aligning the objectives of an improvement initiative with the personal objectives of the managers involved. Without such alignment, they may have little incentive to throw their weight behind a project; the downside for them is that they risk failure or alienation from their peer group, whereas there is little upside in terms of short-term benefits if they succeed.

If John Wexford takes a pragmatic decision to sit on the fence and see how things turn out, the rest of Arboria may well think he is half-hearted about the effort. Taking their cue from him, they could easily conclude that they don't need to give it their full support either.

Ideally, senior managers should be united, committed to the operations improvement programme and prepared to make a personal investment in it. The situation at the Bolton plant is far from ideal. John has refused Philip's request that Dave be the full-time leader of the diagnostic work. Although he may be right that Dave's skills are not best suited to the job, he might not have thought about the strong signal that assigning him to the team would have sent to the organisation.

John's role is critical: as the senior manager at Bolton, he is the plant's principal role model. He has agreed to invest half a day of his management team's time in reviewing the findings, but this is less than Philip wanted. Since a full-time project team will carry out most of the analysis, line managers could easily turn into spectators, not participants. John may believe his team are as clear about the direction and priorities for the plant as he is, but he may be mistaken. His leadership style doesn't encourage people to share different perspectives, so opportunities to explore issues within the team are rare.

In such circumstances, it can be helpful to involve an independent outsider as a facilitator. Their role is to gain the trust of each person in a team in order to understand where points of divergence may lie and then to put these differences on the table without unduly exposing any individual.

For now, though, the ball is in Philip's court as he sets out to assess the plant's operations and the scope for improvement.

The day after his meeting with John, Philip spoke to all the members of the team that would be conducting the diagnostic and agreed their participation with their managers. There was so little opposition from their managers that he was left wondering whether he really had the best team for the job. He was nevertheless pleased to be starting the work he had been hired to do at last.

The team was to consist of Christine McGuire from production planning, who understood the intricacies of the scheduling system; Fiona Richardson, the team leader from the coffee machine assembly line; Derek Hines, a senior maintenance engineer from the mould shop; and two production engineers, Lisa Hallum and Steve Edwards (see Figure 7.4). Philip also arranged with Brian Johnson, Bolton's finance manager, to have two days a week of the factory accountant's time during the diagnostic. Since Dave couldn't take part, Philip would lead the team himself and share in the work. He arranged for the training room to be cleared of prototypes and other paraphernalia so that they could use it as their base.

Lean Diagnostic Team

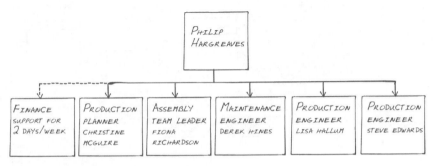

Figure 7.4 Lean diagnostic team

The following Monday morning, Philip assembled his team in the training room and outlined his plan. He began by stressing the importance of not getting lost in the detail, and explained that they would use the MIFA to maintain a systems view.

'There's no mystery about MIFA; all it does is give us a way of describing the whole value stream from start to finish on one piece of paper', he explained. 'It forces us to take a bird's-eye view of the process and helps us understand the interactions between the material flow – making stuff – and the information flow, which tells us what to make, how much to make and when.'

Despite Philip's enthusiasm, the team were looking a bit lost. To help them, he quickly sketched a MIFA diagram on the electronic whiteboard (see Figure 7.5). He explained how information flowed from the customer through Arboria and back to its suppliers of parts and raw materials. He

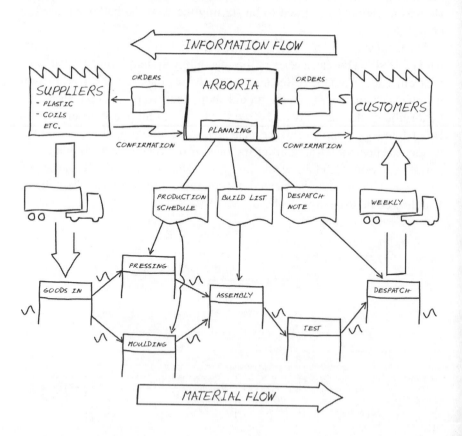

Figure 7.5 Philip's MIFA sketch

then showed how material flowed in the opposite direction, ending with the delivery of finished goods to customers.

'This end-to-end material flow is the value stream we'll be working on. In between the material flow and the information flow is production planning, which tries to translate the customer's requirements into the instructions that prompt the production of the right products in the right quantity at the right time.'

'*Tries* being the operative word,' muttered Fiona.

Christine rose to the bait. 'I can't help it if customers can't make up their mind what they want.'

Philip ignored the interruption. 'What we'll see is that there are good reasons why we struggle to get products out of the door on time. As we identify the root causes of these difficulties, we'll be able to set out a logical plan to put these things right.'

Rather than muddy the waters by going into more detail, Philip decided to set the team to work. He showed them a list he'd drawn up of the seven steps to map the current state (see Figure 7.6).

'We'll do the first few steps in parallel. I suggest we pair up so that someone who knows each part of a particular value stream is working with someone who can bring a fresh perspective to it. So, Christine and Lisa, can you start by looking at true customer demand data on a weekly basis by product number for the past 12 months? Derek and Fiona, I'd like you to gather production, changeover and reliability data for the moulding machines based on what really happens. If you get the chance, try to note down the stock levels for each product too. Steve and I will spend some

Seven steps to create a MIFA

1. Customer requirements
2. Process steps
3. Process data
4. Inventory
5. Material flow from supplier to customer
6. Information flow (push or pull)
7. Lead time and value-added time

arboria®

Figure 7.6 Seven steps to create a MIFA

time in the assembly areas gathering data on the way work is allocated currently.'

'Do you mean the stock levels in the warehouse or out in the factory?' asked Fiona.

'Good question. We need both. In fact, wherever there is inventory, note down the quantity and the location. If the same product number is stored in several places, we need to know. Remember – and this goes for everything we do as a team over the next few weeks – don't take what people tell you as gospel, or trust what you read in a report. Go and see for yourself. That's the golden rule.'

'We'll be popular!' Derek commented.

'I realise we may have to tread on a few toes,' Philip replied. 'But we've got to get at what really happens. We're bound to find a few skeletons in the cupboard.'

'Don't get me wrong, Philip. It's got to be the right thing for the business. All I'm saying is, don't expect everyone to thank you for it.' Derek cast a knowing glance at Christine.

Clutching notebooks and pencils, the team set off in search of data.

Evaluating the Operating System

Philip is using MIFA to structure the team's thinking and force them to work at a higher level than their roles usually allow. MIFA won't provide all the answers but it will give them a way into the problem, helping them to identify root causes of waste and pinpoint the areas that need more detailed analysis. The interaction that MIFA tracks – that between information flow and materials flow – is in itself one of the most common sources of loss in an operating system.

One company that made customised parts for the construction industry used MIFA to assess its operating system. It had such a big problem with slow-moving finished goods inventory that it was running out of space to store it. The root cause turned out to be late changes to customer delivery dates caused by a range of factors, such as bad weather delaying work at building sites. The changes were often made after the products had been launched to production.

To try to overcome this problem, an employee would phone customers on the Wednesday before delivery to check whether they still needed the products they had ordered. Although not part of the formal scheduling process, this role was probably one of the most important at the site, as the MIFA analysis revealed. This insight led to the recognition that shorter manufacturing lead times were the key to reducing inventory. If orders were launched to production much later, the phone call would be effective in filtering out the production of unwanted orders. Within two months, the piles of products on the shop floor had virtually disappeared.

Arboria has similar difficulty in translating constantly changing customer requirements into production instructions. At present, it handles orders centrally at head office before sending them on to the plants, which may be part of the problem; additional stages in the supply chain tend to amplify demand swings. Whatever the cause, Arboria must improve its performance, since one of the objectives of the lean transformation is to make the plants more flexible and responsive to customers and thereby gain a genuine advantage over competitors from outside Europe.

When studying the value stream from end to end, you need to set limits to the scope of your diagnosis. Philip's evaluation of the operating system is limited to the Bolton site since he believes business needs can be addressed by working at this level. But sometimes diagnostic teams have to cast their net wider.

At one centre for processing loan applications, staff had to scan application forms so that they could be stored electronically. Because the forms came from brochures, the staff had to slit the pages and remove staples before putting them in the automated scanner. This created a huge amount of unnecessary work for a centre handling thousands of applications a day. In this case, the end-to-end view had to extend beyond the processing centre to the branches in order to treat the root cause of this particular source of loss.

As they walked over to the coffee machine assembly area, Philip explained his plans to Steve. 'We're going to follow a part through the assembly process. Imagine you are a customer waiting for a particular coffee machine. Watch it as it flows along the value stream, and keep asking yourself, am I willing to pay for that activity?'

'I'm not sure I understand. Are you talking about the activities the assembly operators carry out?'

'Yes, but also everything else that happens to a part, whether it's two components being put together, or a box of mouldings being moved, or the rework on a coffee machine that has failed a test. Whenever anything happens to the part, ask whether it is adding value or just cost. If it's cost, we should ask what we can do to eliminate that source of loss.'

'I see.'

'There are two ways to affect profitability: price and cost. The business can do a bit to influence price, but essentially the market sets it. Cost, on the other hand, is largely within our control. If we can find and plug cost leaks, we'll increase our profitability.'

As they approached the assembly area, Philip tugged Steve's sleeve. 'Hang on. Let's just pause here and watch for a minute.'

Four operators were at work in the coffee machine assembly area. The first checked the main moulding for defects and fitted the level indicator. The second fitted the heating element and seal, assembled the switch and control panel, and threaded the wires up through the housing to the indicator lamps. All the electrical components were supplied to the line pre-assembled.

The third operator then turned the assembly over, applied glue to the underside of the main housing, and pressed the base into place using a pneumatic press. The fourth person tested the coffee machine in an electrical test fixture before putting it into a bag with an instruction leaflet and assembling a printed flat-packed box to put it in.

'What do you think?' asked Philip.

'It looks OK at first glance. Everyone's busy. There's plenty going on.'

'What about when you follow a single part with the eye of a customer?'

Steve watched the first operator, who had noticed by now that she was being observed. She finished working on the part and put it down on the table next to her, alongside several others.

'Well, my part isn't being worked on now, but that's not really adding cost, is it?'

'Maybe not cost, but it is adding time,' Philip replied. 'Imagine we're watching not a coffee machine but a product that goes off, like fruit. We need to think of our products as perishable, and work at getting them through the process as fast as we can so they arrive fresh at the customer. Imagine the smell from all that fruit going off because it's hanging around in here doing nothing.'

'I suppose that's true in a way,' Steve said thoughtfully. 'If we're going to respond more quickly to customers' needs, we can't afford to have product tied up in the process just waiting to be worked on. It all adds to the lead time.'

'Exactly! Keep watching your part. What happens next?'

Steve watched as the second woman, who looked a little uneasy, worked with impressive dexterity on the product. She then put it on the assembly table next to her work area, where once again there were several part-assembled coffee machines waiting to be glued. The gluing station operator was poking the pneumatic press with a screwdriver as though he were trying to free something caught inside. Meanwhile, the backlog was mounting.

'Looks like the gluing station is playing up again', said Steve. 'We know all about that; it's on our list.'

'You can see the effect it has on the flow of work, can't you? The unreliability of the press creates variability that leads to waste elsewhere in the process while the upstream operators wait for the backlog to clear. The guy on the test station has run out of parts to test, so look what he's doing now.'

The fourth operator was making up cardboard boxes and stacking them next to the test machine.

'Surely it makes sense for him to use the time productively?' asked Steve.

'Of course, but he doesn't actually *need* the boxes right now. I'm not blaming him; he means well, but he's overproducing.'

'It's quite an eye-opener,' Steve admitted.

'The boxes take up space and make the area harder to move around in. Meanwhile, the real problem with the gluing machine hasn't gone away, though it's partly hidden because the operator's keeping himself busy with other things.'

'I'm just going to check that Fiona and Derek are OK in the mould shop. It would be great if you could note down how long it takes to complete each operation to give us data on work content. Just use the second hand on your watch. Back in a minute.' Philip headed off.

Steve rested his notebook on a pallet of flat-packed boxes next to the assembly area and took his watch off. He noted how long the first operator took to complete the cycle of work: 24 seconds, 26 seconds, 33 seconds ...

'What this? Time and motion?' asked Jeff Aspinall, who was packing the coffee machines.

'No, nothing like that. We just need to know how long it takes to build a coffee machine from start to finish.'

'Who's "we"?'

'Well, Philip Hargreaves, the new lean implementation manager. He was here a minute ago.'

'Oh yes. What's "lean" then?'

By now the others had stopped work and gathered round. Steve felt uncomfortable: it hadn't been a good idea to start observing activities without first explaining what he was doing to the production team. As they fired questions at him, he realised he was out of his depth. He made his excuses and left, but he knew the damage had been done.

He found Philip in the mould shop and explained what had happened. Fiona offered to go back and talk to the team. Philip was annoyed with himself for letting this happen. He should have briefed the team properly; he'd got carried away when the opportunity came up to coach Steve.

As they walked back, Fiona tried to reassure Steve. 'Don't worry, love, they'll be all right once we explain what we're doing. It's just that nobody tells us anything on the line, and after a while you get fed up with being treated like mushrooms.'

'Mushrooms?'

'Kept in the dark and covered in shit.'

Fiona smoothed things over with the assembly team and Steve apologised for not explaining that he was trying to understand the process, not check up on individuals. Once everyone had calmed down, they were curious to find out more, and started volunteering ideas for improvements. After promising to take their ideas on board and share the diagnostic findings with them, Fiona went back to the mould shop, leaving Steve timing the rest of the process.

At the end of the day, the team got together to review progress. The initial findings were revealing. Steve had discovered that not only did the average times for the four processes differ, but also there was considerable variation within each process. The net effect was that, on average, operators spent about half their time waiting.

Fiona explained that many machines in the mould shop seemed to have utilisation of over 100 per cent, but this was because the cycle times had a built-in allowance for changeovers and breakdowns. From the rough estimates that she and Derek had made, the true figure was probably more like 70 per cent if calculated as the actual output of good parts divided by the theoretical output, or shift time divided by machine cycle time.

'We have to make allowances for breakdowns and changeovers in our planning assumptions to be realistic about what we'll actually get from a run,' Christine explained.

'But you can see the problem,' said Philip. 'By measuring machine effectiveness that way, you're hiding its true potential.'

'I'm not sure that's right,' Derek replied. 'If we didn't include an allowance for breakdowns, we'd be in a right mess.'

'Just think about it, Derek,' Philip continued. 'Why do we *allow* breakdowns? Doesn't the language we use betray our attitude? It's as though we expect breakdowns to happen, and even plan for them.'

'How else could we do it?' Christine asked.

'It's important to separate production planning from performance monitoring,' Philip replied. 'For planning purposes, we need to recognise that our machines aren't as reliable as they might be, and make some allowance to protect the customer. But when we're looking at performance, we have to uncover the full potential; otherwise we're setting an artificial limit on improvement. If people see 100 per cent utilisation, they think everything's fine, but if our figures are correct, there's another 30 per cent improvement that stays hidden. Just think, we might invest hundreds of thousands of pounds in a new machine because we think we're short of capacity when in fact there's plenty to spare; we just can't get at it yet.'

Philip could see that the team were beginning to understand; they were learning to see their processes from a customer's perspective. As they shared what they had learnt and explored the problems that had surfaced after just a few hours' work, their energy and enthusiasm grew.

Interpreting the Findings

When the team complete the MIFA, they will use it to find out what additional analyses they need to perform to understand the implications of customer demand. It will also help them quantify the theoretical potential of various options such as eliminating waiting time on the assembly line or reducing the time lost through machine breakdowns in the mould shop.

Customer Demand

The assessment and design of the operating system needs to start from customer demand. Understanding its level, mix and variability is crucial. Many Arboria products are bought as gifts, and about 40 per cent of annual sales occur in the fourth quarter running up to Christmas. With demand exceeding capacity at this time of year, products are stockpiled on the basis of Christmas sales forecasts.

The one thing you can guarantee about a forecast is that it will be wrong; the only question is by how much. If Arboria over-estimates demand, unsold stock will be left in the supply chain at the end of the season. If it isn't piled high in Arboria's warehouse, it will be cleared at discount prices by the retailers.

In the past, the company invested heavily in computer models to improve the accuracy of its forecasts, but saw little benefit. What it should be doing is trying to increase the effective capacity of its plants so that it can shift from 'make to stock' to 'make to order'. That way, it will deliver what customers really want, not what it thinks they want.

Such an approach will throw up other issues, such as how to handle the surplus capacity that has been released during the off season, and how to create more flexible working arrangements so that employees can work more when the business needs them and less when it doesn't. These issues aren't easy to resolve, since they cut across many aspects of the business from purchasing to sales, and personnel management to manufacturing. That's why it is so critical for the whole management team to be aligned around the effort and its objectives.

Equipment Utilisation

The operational data gathered in the diagnostic needs to be translated into financial benefits, whether they are bottom-line gains or savings from deferred investments. At Arboria, the introduction of new products and colours had put strain on its production capacity, especially in mouldings. Management had been debating whether to subcontract some of the mouldings or invest in new capacity. The diagnostic team have uncovered a third option: to release latent capacity from existing assets so that planned investments can be postponed or abandoned. This could have a huge impact on Arboria's ROCE; indeed, in capital-intensive processes, the release of latent capacity is often the single biggest driver of the financial benefits that accrue from a lean transformation.

Measuring performance rigorously leaves no hiding place for losses. If it replaced its current method of calculating machine utilisation with a more robust measure, Arboria would have a basis for assessing real performance levels and setting improvement targets. Many organisations now use overall equipment effectiveness (OEE) and similar measures to monitor their assets, since these take account of the so-called six big losses: breakdowns, changeovers, speed losses, minor stops, quality defects and process spoilage.

A steel foundry whose performance hadn't shifted for several years used OEE data as the basis for conducting a limit analysis. A consultant pushed the team to imagine what the theoretical limit to improving any loss might be. If it took ten minutes to discharge and reload a vessel, could a little extra investment reduce this to four minutes if everything ran like clockwork? Four minutes didn't become the improvement target (indeed, it might not even be attainable), but the team set an objective to halve the gap with the theoretical limit over the next 12 months. By adopting this approach, the steel foundry made a step-change in performance that the workforce didn't believe was possible at the outset.

Labour Productivity

Philip and Steve's observations and the data Steve subsequently gathered reveal there is a huge opportunity to improve labour productivity on the assembly line. To capture it, Arboria will need to standardise operations to reduce variability and then reallocate the work content evenly between the operators (sometimes called 'balancing the line'). When it does this, it needs to know what *rate* of production the work needs to be balanced *to*.

The obvious thing to do would be to take the total amount of work on the coffee maker line and divide it equally between the four operators. This will certainly enable the product to flow more smoothly along the line. However, the flow will probably now be faster than the rate at which the customer requires the product (the *Takt* time).

The correct approach is first to determine the *Takt* time for the product, and then to divide the total work content by the *Takt* time to determine how many operators are needed. This ensures that only the labour required to meet customer needs is allocated to the product. When the rate of demand changes, as it does during the fourth quarter, the number of operators will also need to change.

One of the benefits of creating simple visual standards for each operation early in the lean transformation is that they provide a basis for reallocating the work between operators when the *Takt* time changes. Such standards also help improve quality and reduce variability in cycle time, and create the conditions for continuous improvement as waste is removed from the process and standards are updated to the improved condition.

Lead Time

One of the most revealing pieces of information that comes out of the MIFA is the actual lead time, together with the amount of value-added time expressed as a percentage of the total lead time. Total lead time is defined as the time it takes for one product to make its way from the start of the value stream to the end through the normal processing routing.

Suppose a garage takes 30 minutes to give a car a basic service. If there are ten cars outside the garage waiting to be serviced and another four inside, then the total lead time for the customer is 7.5 hours: 7 hours when the car is waiting (14 cars multiplied by the 30-minute cycle time), plus half an hour for the actual service. Now imagine a video camera is recording a complete service. When the video is analysed, it turns out that the time spent working on the car in ways that add value to the customer – such as removing the old filters and fitting new ones – is only about five minutes. This means that the value-added time (five minutes divided by 7.5 hours) is only about 1 per cent.

In Arboria's case, the MIFA revealed that the proportion of value-added time was actually a fraction of 1 per cent. Although this might sound staggering (and will probably be greeted with disbelief by management when the team share their findings), it isn't really so surprising, since the quantity of inventory in the process drives the figure down. Many businesses carry a lot of work in progress to help them respond to changes in customer demand, but it actually has the opposite effect.

Inventory should be thought of as a queue that moves slowly forward, one unit at a time, as the last item is delivered to the customer. The right way to build flexibility is to drive this inventory down to the lowest level capable of maintaining flow. Work in progress is like oil in an engine: you need enough to lubricate all the moving parts, but no more.

Imagine that our garage redesigns its operating system to eliminate inventory (so there is no need to pre-book) and cut out waste (so the service takes just 15 minutes). In doing so, it creates a new business model that will serve the market segment of drivers who can't or don't want to plan their service in advance. At the same time, the garage has doubled its effective capacity, thus opening up the opportunity to double revenues. Simple though this example is, many businesses, including McDonald's and Dell are based on similar principles. Because such models leave little room for variability, clear operating standards are imperative.

Arboria must apply the same approach to reduce its inventory levels to the bare minimum needed to service customers. In this way, it will not only become more responsive to customers, but also reduce the working capital in the business and cut the cost of writing off obsolete stock each year.

Gaps in the Assessment

Before we go back to Arboria, let's consider the diagnostic that Philip and the team have carried out. They've made a thorough assessment of the key aspects of the operating system and identified important shortfalls in performance management, such as the machine utilisation measure. But if we take as our yardstick the three dimensions of operating system, management infrastructure and mindsets and behaviour, there are clearly gaps.

Although Philip and the team have addressed some aspects of performance management, they haven't made a systematic assessment of the whole performance management cycle. They haven't considered whether people's personal objectives are linked into operational objectives; nor have they assessed the degree of multi-skilling that exists within the workforce, which could be central to an improved operating system. Nor has Philip chosen to carry out a formal review of the organ-isation structure, since he feels he lacks the mandate and the credibility to do so.

If a lean transformation doesn't include an assessment of management infrastructure and mindsets and behaviours, it risks being seen as a techni-cal effort managed by technical people. Coming from a business where lean was part of the furniture, Philip has underestimated the gap between the management team's current level of understanding and what it needs to make the change happen.

The incident when the assembly operators reacted against being observed testifies to a disempowered workforce who have become accustomed to having things done to them. The diagnostic presents an ideal opportunity to make a break with the past and reconnect management with the reality of the front line. For now, it looks as though this is an opportunity Arboria has missed.

The day of the workshop with the plant management team has arrived. John's team, including Philip, have held their usual monthly review in the morning. Now the diagnostic team has joined them for sandwiches. Some of the team have never been in the boardroom before, and find it daunting.

'OK everyone, we're running a bit behind, so anyone who needs a coffee to stay awake, grab one now. Phil, over to you.'

Philip was taken aback. He'd asked John in advance if he would outline the reasons for the diagnostic, and John had agreed. Maybe it had slipped his mind, or maybe he'd decided to dispense with the formalities to save time.

'Er, thanks, John,' Philip said. 'Well, as I think you all know, ExCo has decided to undertake a transformation of Arboria's operations. Bruno and Dietmar asked me to take the lead in carrying out an assessment here, and then report back to ExCo at next week's European Leadership Meeting. That's what this team has been up to for the past three weeks, and now we want to share our findings and hear what you think. I hope we can make it more of a discussion than a presentation. So, if there aren't any questions for now, over to you, Fiona.'

'Thanks, Philip.'

As she walked over to the huge MIFA diagram that the team had stuck on the wall, Fiona looked self-conscious; she'd never done anything like this before. The diagram showed every process and every material and information flow in the coffee maker value stream.

Fiona explained what the MIFA had revealed, and the management team, clearly intrigued, asked questions that Fiona either answered herself or passed to others in the team. After a while, Philip brought the discussion to a close and summed up what they had learned.

'The main things we wanted to get across are that the way we do things now is very complicated, and that there are lots of points in the value stream where things don't quite connect. This creates waste, or leaks, if you like. Although it sounds like bad news, it means there's a huge opportunity for us to improve by plugging these leaks and making the product flow through the value stream more efficiently.'

'How would you do that?' Brian Johnson asked.

'Well, I don't want to jump the gun because we've got a lot more to show you, but basically it would mean that we start to pull the product through the system based on actual orders, rather than push it through based on a forecast as we do today', Philip replied. 'Before we get ahead of ourselves, I'd like Christine to explain the analysis she and Lisa have done on customer demand.'

Christine put a chart on the overhead projector showing the monthly demand for coffee maker products. It looked reasonably smooth, but rose in the fourth quarter.

'As you can see, the graph looks quite smooth apart from the sales peak in the run-up to Christmas. But when you look at weekly demand, it's a different story.' She put up another graph showing weekly sales over the past year. The line had the same overall shape, but went up and down much more.

'Is this what we made or what we actually shipped?' asked Dave.

'Neither,' Lisa answered. 'It's data from the sales system showing what the customer ordered for this product family.'

'Why are you looking at that?' he asked.

'Because it shows what the customer really wants. We wanted to start with that and see how it compares to what we actually produced.'

'And what did you find?' Dave was curious.

'Hang on a minute,' said Christine, who had worked with Dave for years. 'Before we look at that, we want to show one more graph, which is the weekly demand by product code, rather than for the whole product family.'

She put up a graph that was full of spikes.

'It looks like the bloody Himalayas,' John said.

'I'm confused,' said Brian. 'What's this telling us?'

Philip tried to explain. 'We wanted to show how much demand varies at the level of a particular product from one week to the next. The graph is spiky because it's so detailed: it takes each product code week by week. It's like increasing the magnification on a microscope. This is the true level of variation we need to be able to deal with. It's only by getting down to this level of detail that we can work out how much finished goods stock we need to hold to protect us from variation.'

'I still don't follow,' Brian said, frowning.

'Neither do I, for that matter,' John added.

Dave chipped in. 'We need to carry enough stock to cover these peaks, otherwise we could be caught with our pants down.'

'Exactly!' said Philip, trying not to laugh. 'Our problem is that at the moment we carry a lot more than that.'

'Is that true?' John asked, turning to Bill.

'Of course. It's because we only make some variants once a month.'

'And that's the point,' said Philip. 'If we made every product every week, we could eliminate over half of our finished goods stock.'

'Now that *is* worth discussing,' said Brian, brightening at the prospect of reducing the cash tied up in stock.

'Hold on!' Bill cut in. 'We've been down this road before and it was a disaster. We were letting customers down left, right and centre. You can't be serious about making every product every week. Do you know how many changeovers that would take?'

'It's true we'd need to cut changeover times, but from what we've seen, that's quite possible.'

Lisa took over and put up a chart on the overhead projector. 'From this analysis, you can see that over 85 per cent of our coffee maker sales comes from just seven products. The other 20 or so products hardly sell, add a lot of complexity to production, and force us to carry additional stocks throughout the process.'

Philip backed her up. 'If we could eliminate these 20 products, we could cut stocks by nearly 50 per cent again, and if we could achieve changeover times of less than 30 minutes, we could make every product every week.'

'I'd like to be part of that conversation,' said Bill. 'I want to know what I'm being committed to. It's downright impossible to make every product every week.'

'OK, we'll take that up afterwards. Let's move on to the next item.'

Fiona and Derek shared their findings from the mould shop. When they announced that the true utilisation of the injection moulding machines was anywhere between 50 per cent and 70 per cent rather than the 100 per cent they had thought, eyebrows were raised and John gave Bill a sideways glance.

Somehow, though, the meeting had gone off the boil after the animated discussion about demand data. By the time Steve came to lay out the data showing that assembly operators spent up to half their time waiting for parts or information, there was little reaction.

Philip drew things to a close by presenting the team's estimate of the savings Arboria could achieve by addressing the losses they had identified. If the findings from the coffee maker line held true for the rest of the business, the cost base of £40 million could be reduced by as much as 15 or 20 per cent. This did provoke a response.

'Bloody hell!' John burst out. 'That seems unbelievable. You'll need to take me through the detail later, Philip. Once Bruno sees those figures, they'll be baked into the budget for next year just like mushrooms in a pizza!'

The others laughed, but John wasn't entirely joking. Bruno's eyes would light up at numbers like these: they would help him deliver the stronger bottom-line performance that the US parent company wanted. It would be important to manage his expectations, and those of ExCo. The upcoming European leadership meeting on 16 June presented an excellent opportunity to do just that.

Communicating the Findings

Although Philip felt the meeting went well overall, he was left with a few concerns. Because of his failure to involve the management team in the analysis itself, the diagnostic team had had to share a mass of information, some of it controversial, in a short time. The details had seemed to go over managers' heads. Perhaps it would have been more effective to hold weekly reviews, or to syndicate the findings to individual managers before the formal debrief with the whole team.

By adopting a different approach, the team might have forestalled some of the difficulties they encountered when they suggested simplifying the product range and making every product every week. For Bill, who hasn't been involved in analysing an area for which he is responsible, the suggestion is like a red rag to a bull. As planning manager, he may feel he will lose his authority if scheduling is simplified in this way. Whatever the business benefits may be, convincing Bill to work in a different way looks like being a challenge.

Though the management team didn't follow some of the technical implications of the analysis, they were quick to grasp the financial implications. John realised he needed to spend more time with Philip on the logic and the detail behind the figures, otherwise he might find himself asked to commit to something he didn't understand. John and Bill also decided they needed to understand the implications of the work on customer demand before the presentation to ExCo. Understandably, they are keen to avoid being misrepresented by a newcomer to the organisation, particularly since his role seems to include assessing how well things have been done in the past.

Philip knew that challenging assumptions and changing habits would be tricky. Designing a new operating system on paper doesn't alter anything; to make things happen, people need to work together. Earlier in his career, Philip had worked for a Texan, and he'd never forgotten one of his favourite routines.

'Five birds are sitting on a wire and three decide to fly south. How many are left?'

'Two,' Philip had said warily.

'Wrong!' his boss had crowed. 'Five! Three of them might have decided to fly south, but they ain't done nothing about it yet.'

CHAPTER 8

Engaging the Leadership

- The leadership team must be aligned around a clear end state with measurable objectives that are linked to business needs.
- Leaders must develop a coherent and compelling 'change story' to communicate both the desired end state and the path leading there to their workforce.
- The implementation must be thoroughly planned, including an assessment of management talent and the assignment of roles to key stakeholders.

Philip's team has now carried out a thorough assessment of the operations for the coffee maker product group at Arboria's Bolton plant. It revealed that there is considerable scope for improvement provided fundamental changes can be made to the operating system. But the local management team still has only a limited understanding of the issues. Part of the reason is that they haven't been directly involved in carrying out the diagnostic.

If the journey to lean is to be successful, the leadership needs to define the target end state, develop plans to achieve it, and engage the wider organisation in turning these plans into reality. The definition of the target state begins with the operating system: the material and information flows and associated people processes needed to satisfy overall business objectives. The definition is produced by breaking down high-level objectives such as ROCE into operational performance targets, such as equipment utilisation, that the future-state operating system must be able to deliver.

The process of developing a shared understanding of the target state is at least as important as the solution itself, and plays a crucial part in aligning the leadership team. As well as acting as architects of the change programme, leaders are also responsible for ensuring that the right people are in the right roles to deliver it, and that all of them take personal responsibility for their particular piece of the overall solution.

The next milestone for Arboria is the European Leadership Meeting, where Philip is to present the diagnostic's findings. As the members gather in Brussels, they each bring different expectations and perspectives on the business problem.

Philip hadn't slept well; early starts always had this effect on him. He could have flown out the evening before, but he tries not to spend too many nights away from home. So at five o'clock he left the house without waking his family. He snoozed on the flight over to Brussels, reckoning he needed sleep more than the dry bacon roll on offer. Arboria had changed its travel policy in the past few weeks, and now all European flights had to be economy. Doubtless this more stringent attitude to cost would be evident in the discussions later that day.

Philip woke with a jolt as the plane landed, and was soon heading towards the taxi rank, thinking over the past week. After the management team review, he'd worked with John, Bill and Brian to explore the financial implications of the diagnostic. John became much more comfortable once he understood that the figure Philip had quoted was the maximum improvement potential. They could only establish an actual target once they'd agreed what the future state would look like.

But Bill was still unhappy, not because he disputed Philip's findings but because he could see where things were heading. When Philip sketched out how production could be controlled by the downstream process, rather than centrally, Bill objected, saying that if life was that simple they'd have done it long ago. Philip was troubled by Bill's antagonism. It would be an uphill struggle to transform production without his cooperation.

Meanwhile Bruno, who hadn't slept well either, was on his way to the office. He was under the spotlight from the United States, and for all the wrong reasons. The results for April were worse than expected, and they were now in danger of missing this half's budget. The main culprits were disappointing sales of a new range of juice-making machines and excessive operating costs.

Bruno recalled the budget planning rounds the previous November. He'd berated the general managers at the three plants for their lack of ambition, and insisted they get tough on costs. They had responded by offering to cut costs by a few percentage points year on year. It was becoming increasingly obvious they wouldn't be able to deliver. That wouldn't play well at the parent company. It had always given him a free rein, but he knew it couldn't last if the results didn't pick up soon.

As he had meetings the day before, John had stayed overnight in a hotel in the centre of Brussels. Dietmar had joined him for dinner, and was keen to know all about the lean diagnostic.

Checking out of the hotel next morning, John couldn't help smiling when the receptionist gave him his bill. How typical: just as the manufacturing plants funded head office, it was he, not Dietmar, who had paid for last night's dinner.

He walked out through the revolving door. Outside, the doorman waved a taxi over from the rank and John got in, heading for the office.

Recognising Different Perspectives

Although Bruno, Dietmar, John and Philip are all on their way to the same meeting, each brings with him a different outlook. To a large extent, their different roles account for this variation in perspective, but differences in character, working style and experience also have a significant influence.

Bruno is accountable for the results of the business, and hopes the lean transformation will generate short-term savings as well as long-term competitive advantage. Dietmar has functional responsibility for operations and wants to understand not just the findings of the diagnostic but also the process, since the plants in Germany and Italy will need to repeat it at some stage. As for John, he is still feeling his way even after his working sessions with Philip, and so is cautious about committing himself to things he may not fully understand.

Aware that Bruno and Dietmar will be assessing whether he is the right person to do the job, Philip is nervous about the meeting. He is also worried about Bill. If key people refuse to change the way they work, there is little chance that Arboria will reach the targets he has set out.

The management team will need opportunities to explore their different perspectives. This requires a certain level of trust, which may have to be built up over time. Take John; experience has taught him to be careful about what he says in front of Bruno, who has a habit of leaping on an unguarded remark. If John continues to feel inhibited about expressing his views, the team's ability to design and lead an effective change programme will be impaired.

We rejoin the team as the meeting begins.

Philip arrived at the office just before nine o' clock, and paid the taxi driver. Seeing Bruno entering the building, he ran over to catch up.

'Hello, Bruno. How are you?'

'Philip! I am quite good.'

'Only *quite* good?'

'I'm sure you've seen the results for April. You don't need me to tell you that we're attracting the wrong kind of attention from our friends in the United States.' He smiled. 'Anyway, I'm counting on you to bring good news.'

'Absolutely,' Philip replied as they got into the lift. 'Our diagnostic shows there's plenty of potential at the plant, but it will mean some big changes to the way we do things.'

'Of course. That's just what we need. What did you find?'

'Well, if we change the way we schedule production to suit what the customer actually requires, we could cut stock levels and lead times by over 50 per cent.'

'Excellent. And this is by using the *kanban* system?'

'Yes.' Philip was taken aback.

'You didn't expect such expert knowledge?' Bruno grinned. 'Remember Dietmar organised a visit for ExCo to the ATC plant a few months ago.'

'Yes, I remember you telling me when I met you both in Brussels.'

'I keep the pictures from that day in here,' Bruno said, tapping his head.

'A very good place to keep them,' Philip replied. The lift stopped and they got out.

'I have some things to do before our meeting at half past nine. You know where to go?' Bruno asked. 'It's down the corridor on the right.'

Philip found the boardroom and plugged his laptop into a cable linked to a ceiling-mounted projector. He was still fiddling with the remote control when Dietmar came in. He greeted Philip warmly and offered to help.

'Why are these things always incompatible?' Philip complained. 'It's infuriating.'

'It's just the same at the plants,' said Dietmar. 'We waste so much time setting up all the different machines.'

'Too true. Actually, that's one of the things we looked at in the diagnostic.'

'I'm looking forward to hearing about it. John was very positive when we spoke last night.'

By this time a few others had come in, though most stayed only long enough to dump their papers on the table. Philip could hear beans being ground in the coffee machine outside.

Half past nine came and went, but the meeting showed no sign of starting. Philip took the chance to introduce himself to the people he hadn't yet met. As he manoeuvred his way back towards the screen, he passed John, who was sitting halfway down the long table. He leaned over and asked him whether such delays were normal.

'Afraid so, Phil, it's always like this. The meeting can't start until Bruno's here, and he's usually the last to arrive.'

Looking annoyed, Dietmar set off to find the latecomers. Ten minutes later, they were finally ready to start. Bruno welcomed everyone and handed straight over to Philip.

By now, Philip was used to these terse introductions, so he got straight to the point, leading the group through the diagnostic findings. For today's meeting, he'd summarised the material from the review with the plant management team. Instead of putting up the MIFA diagram, he used a much simpler version to structure his presentation, outlining the main findings and pinpointing the principal causes of leaks in the value stream.

He'd asked Lisa to film a machine changeover with his digital video camera, and showed the video clip to illustrate examples of waste in the process and share ideas for eliminating it. When he explained that the changeover time for the mould machine could probably be reduced from a couple of hours to less than 30 minutes with very little investment, his audience's interest was palpable. As he drew to the end, his mobile phone rang to the tune of *Mission Impossible*. He apologised and turned it off, embarrassed.

Bruno stepped in. 'Don't worry, Philip. It's a good time to take a break anyway. Thank you. You've helped us see we are sitting on a gold mine. Now it's up to us to get the gold out of the ground. Tell me, have you prepared anything on the next steps?'

'Yes. I've done some thinking about the future-state operating system that I want to share.'

'Very good. Let's take a short break – ten minutes only, everyone – and then restart.'

The meeting broke up and Philip checked his voicemail. It was his wife.

'It's me. Sorry to call you at work like this. It's Robin; he's had an accident. The school's just rung. He was fooling about at break and fell off a

wall and was knocked unconscious. He's been taken to hospital. I'm on my way now. I know you've got a big meeting today, but I'd really like you here. Give me a call as soon as you can.'

Imagining the worst, Philip felt dreadful. A clap on the back brought him back to the boardroom.

'Well done, Phil. Great job.' John noticed the look on his face. 'Are you all right?'

'Not really. That was my wife. My son's had an accident at school. He's been taken to hospital.'

'Good God!' said John. 'You'd better get home. I'll get one of the secretaries to find you a flight. Give me your ticket.'

After Philip left, the mood was sombre. Seeing that people found it hard to concentrate, Bruno suggested they take an early lunch and resume at one o'clock.

Moving from Current-State Findings to Future-State Design

As well as changing the tone of the meeting, Philip's sudden departure poses a problem for the leadership team. They now have a reasonable understanding of the diagnostic findings, but Philip hasn't had time to cover the future-state operating system, and John lacks the knowledge to fill in. Though unexpected, this turn of events could benefit the team in the long run; they'll be forced to discuss the future state between themselves, albeit without the technical detail that Philip would have supplied.

Philip needs to make a transition from being the expert who tells everyone what needs to be done to engaging the team in the problem solving. This crucial step in the change journey is often missed. Senior teams who are already overloaded may delegate the design of the future state to an internal specialist like Philip, or to external consultants. Either is risky. An internal specialist may be tempted to define the end state in exclusively technical terms: lead times, batch sizes, line configuration and so on. And using external consultants may let the management team off the hook: if they don't play an active role, how can they be fully committed to making tough decisions, or realise what they need to change in their own way of working?

A simple way to think about the stages people need to go through before they are committed to changing the way they behave is the '3Es': **explore** (understand the need for change and share perspectives on possible solutions), **engage** (work together to define the vision and agree specific roles and targets) and **enact** (turn the vision into reality and assess progress against targets).

In trying to make change happen quickly, many organisations skip the first two stages and simply tell people: 'Here's the solution, now you implement it.' Since the people who need to change the way they work probably won't understand the solution or be committed to making it happen, this is often counterproductive.

ExCo's visit to ATC, which clearly made an impression on Bruno, exemplifies the 'explore' stage: it helped the senior team grasp the nature of the performance gap and see where their change journey might be leading. The 'engage' stage is about involving people in developing solutions themselves rather than imposing them from above or entrusting them to an expert, which might have happened at the meeting if Philip hadn't been called away. Going through the first two stages makes people far more likely to enact a solution, since they themselves have played a part in shaping it.

When a leadership team engages in defining a future state, the way the team works together may well come under scrutiny. Consider the patterns that are beginning to emerge in the way meetings are run at Arboria. Like the plant review meeting, the European Leadership Meeting starts late and seems to lack clear objectives and outcomes. Coming from a more disciplined organisation, Philip expects it to have a definite structure, with Bruno explaining the reason for the diagnostic and the purpose of reviewing it as a group. As when John chaired the earlier meeting, that didn't happen. Moreover, the behaviour of the leaders is mirrored throughout the organisation. Bruno is always late for meetings, so nobody feels they have to turn up on time.

Even if Philip had been able to present his ideas for a future-state operating system it would have been only the starting point, since the whole leadership team need to agree the definition. As well as redesigning production processes to create flow and minimise losses, they also need to look at the implications for related functions within the operating system, such as product design, maintenance and engineering. In addition, they must define the management infrastructure and mindsets and behaviours needed to sustain the changes.

Bruno and the ExCo have already seen the future on their visit to the ATC plant. But because John and other people at the meeting haven't had this experience, the team as a whole doesn't yet share any reference points.

Later that day, when John was on his way back to the airport, his mobile rang. It was Philip.

'Hello, Phil. How's your lad?'

'He's concussed and he'll be off school for a few days, but he's OK. It'll teach him not to fall off walls.'

'Glad it's not serious. The meeting was like a bloody funeral after you left.'

'I'm sorry I had to dash away.'

'We'd all have done the same. At least your boy waited until you'd done your presentation before he fell off the wall.'

Philip laughed. 'How did the meeting finish?'

'Well, to be honest, it dawned on us that we don't really have much idea where we are trying to get to with this lean thing. We started thinking about the big picture, and realised we hadn't got one.'

'So what did you do?'

'We kicked around a few ideas. In fact, people really opened up. Maybe your boy's accident put things into perspective. Maybe they thought, what the hell? I may as well just say what I think.'

'Sounds productive. So what came out of it?'

'Well, I stressed that we've got far too many products to manage our operations properly. So we talked about the way we currently schedule production, and how consolidating orders centrally amplifies demand swings. We also started to talk about the people side.'

'What do you mean, training?'

'Yes, but also wider issues: the organisation structure, the way we recruit and reward people, the sense of urgency in the organisation – that kind of thing. Believe it or not, we decided that the ExCo members need to spend more time in the plants if they are serious about this lean transformation.'

'Wow! I'm impressed. Sounds like a valuable discussion.'

'It was a revelation. Normally we just skirt around the real issues, partly for lack of time but also because of Bruno. He's a hard taskmaster, and I guess we've all learned to keep things under our hat. Anyway, today was a step in the right direction.'

'Anything else I should know about?'

'No big decisions. We ran out of time. But Bruno said he'd work with ExCo to define the overall business objectives for the programme, as we don't have any yet. He's also coming over to Bolton with Dietmar in a couple of weeks to work with us on defining the future state. He promised the high-level objectives will be defined by then.'

'Fantastic! Maybe it was a good thing I left when I did.'

'One more thing; Bruno kept going on about a plant he visited with ExCo. Do you know anything about it?'

'Yes. They arranged a benchmark visit a while back to get a better understanding of lean.'

'Right. Could we do something similar to give us a better idea of where we're heading? I feel we're still groping in the dark.'

'Absolutely. I should be able to arrange a visit to my old plant, unless you were thinking of something else.'

'Sounds great.'

The moment he got off the phone, Philip called his old boss to ask if they could visit. They fixed on the following Friday.

Building Alignment within the Team

One of the prerequisites for exploring different opinions and reaching alignment within a team is trust. Without it, individuals are unlikely to speak up in front of a group and say what they really think. But they may tell a colleague privately; indeed, such corridor conversations are where the real agendas are often shared.

People are even more likely to hold back where the senior figure is highly dominant. Leaders like Bruno provide such a strong steer that dissenting views are frequently perceived as unwelcome, and perhaps even as professional suicide. Through sheer force of character, Bruno is unwittingly preventing important issues from coming to the surface. Other inhibiting factors are also at work here, including the participants' relative status in the corporate hierarchy and the size of the team: over a dozen at the ELM. The larger the meeting, the smaller the chance that the members will be willing to trust everyone else in the group.

However it is done, the top team must become aligned. One approach is for a neutral external party to conduct open-ended interviews with each member of the management team, and then stage a workshop to explore the findings with the whole team while protecting individuals' confidentiality. Such interviews are reflective, free-ranging and informal; rather than imposing a structure, the interviewer elicits what the interviewee thinks is important. The interviews often take two or three hours: long enough to establish a rapport and cut through superficial issues to underlying concerns, which may not come to light until near the end. Any common themes that emerge can be distilled into a set of statements that can be tested with the whole team during a workshop.

At one big company, several members of the senior team observed in interviews that their own team decisions were seldom followed through. During the workshop that followed, members were asked if they agreed with the statement: 'As a team, we act collectively to support team decisions.' Polling technology was used to collate the responses, and the result was displayed on a screen for everyone to discuss. Eight out of 14 members disagreed. It was much easier for them to acknowledge their views within an anonymous process. Such workshops have to be managed carefully so that they work towards positive and constructive outcomes. In such circumstances it's important to use an external facilitator to follow up the issues raised and help the team explore the reasons behind them.

Arboria's leadership team has begun to discuss the key issues that must be addressed before operations can be transformed. Among them is the perception that the members of ExCo spend too little time in the plants. By agreeing to come to Bolton to work with the management team on developing a vision of the future state, Bruno and Dietmar have shown that they take the team's views seriously and are willing to make an effort to change their own working habits.

The visit to Philip's old company, Autoplast, opened the eyes of the management team, some of whom had never been in a manufacturing plant from another industry. Afterwards, they felt they had a much better sense of where they might be heading.

News of the planned workshop with Bruno and Dietmar spread. For several managers at the Bolton plant, it would be their first encounter with Bruno. In his rare visits, he usually stayed away from the shop floor unless customers were visiting.

To prepare for the workshop, John got Philip to brief him on the ideas he had developed for the future state of the operating system. They agreed that the object of the workshop was not to go into detail about how production should be organised, but to lift the discussion to a higher plane and come to a shared view of how the future state would affect the business. If it required a radically different approach to scheduling production and organising maintenance, for instance, the team would need to know what the new way of working might look like so as to understand the implications for them and their subordinates.

John also spent time with Louise Bradley, the plant's personnel manager, discussing the changes that would need to be made to the organisation structure and other issues that had been on his mind. They shared ideas for improving the relationship between production and maintenance and dividing responsibilities between them, and considered whether the two functions should remain separate. The production team leaders were soon identified as the lynchpin of improved operational performance. John and Louise agreed that though the people in these roles had good technical skills, they lacked the capabilities to manage and coach their teams effectively.

The day of the workshop arrived. Having completed the introductions, John set the scene, putting up an agenda and then the objectives for the day (see Figure 8.1).

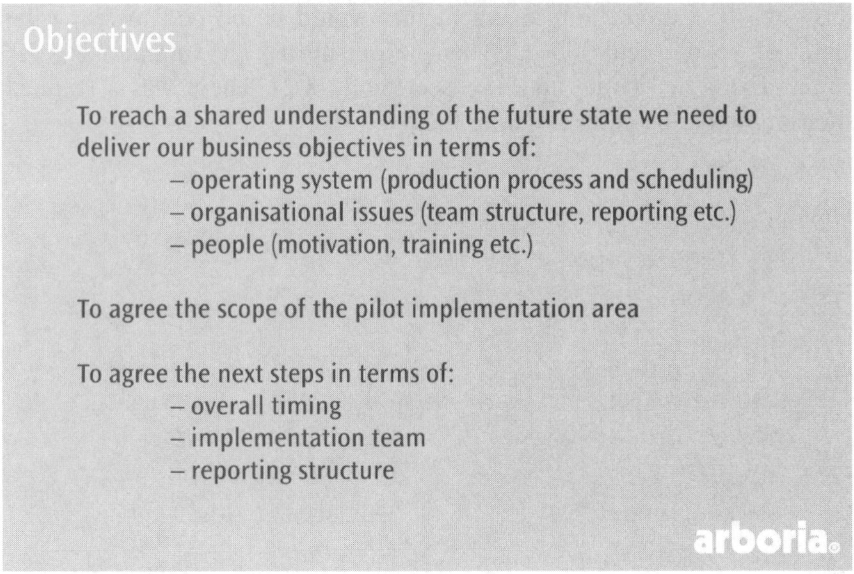

To reach a shared understanding of the future state we need to deliver our business objectives in terms of:
- operating system (production process and scheduling)
- organisational issues (team structure, reporting etc.)
- people (motivation, training etc.)

To agree the scope of the pilot implementation area

To agree the next steps in terms of:
- overall timing
- implementation team
- reporting structure

arboria.

Figure 8.1 Objectives

Bruno scanned the list. 'Good. This is OK for me.'

'Any other comments, anyone?' John asked.

'Yes. Can you explain what you mean by pilot implementation?' asked Bill.

Philip offered to answer. 'Following on from the diagnostic, it probably makes sense to continue with the coffee maker product family. That way we can prove the new operating system in a manageable area of the plant without disrupting the rest of the business. Running a pilot will allow us to test and refine our future-state design, but also show us which other areas are creaking and need strengthening or changing before we implement across the whole site.'

'I see. Thanks.'

'Right, let's move on then, shall we?' said John. 'Bruno? Dietmar? Over to you, guys.'

Bruno began by talking about the wider business and the concerns that he hoped the lean transformation would address. The team were fascinated to hear their CEO talking candidly about Arboria's problems, and the workshop got off to a good start.

Dietmar presented an analysis he had carried out with Jenny, the finance director. It revealed Arboria's rising cost base and eroding margins. He used the ROCE tree developed by Philip and the team to

show the operational improvement that would be needed to reach the
target of 16 per cent ROCE. Then he put up a page summarising the
targets ExCo had come up with (see Figure 8.2). There was a stunned
silence, broken by John exhaling loudly.

Lean programme objectives, 2005

	Q2 2003	Q4 2005
Return on capital employed	8.7%	16%
Sales per employee per year	€125 000	€180 000
Lead time (order to shipment)	3–6 weeks	5 days
On time delivery	93.6%	99%
Warranty returns	4 000 ppm	<300 ppm

arboria.

Figure 8.2 Lean programme objectives, 2005

'We know these are tough targets,' said Dietmar.
'We need to set ourselves ambitious goals,' explained Bruno. 'If we
don't aim high, we won't push ourselves to make a step-change.'
'What do you think, Philip?' asked Dietmar.
'Well, setting aside the ROCE target, which I guess comes from the
United States, I think the operational targets are an enormous stretch but,
basing it on my past experience, feasible none the less. The productivity
target of 18 000 euros looks very tough though. I could imagine making a
20 or even 30 per cent improvement, but that would imply nearly 50
per cent.'
'Yes, but some of it will come from the top line. We've assumed that the
projected sales growth can be absorbed.'
'I see. Then maybe it's possible. But we should probably separate out the
two components of that figure, since the plant can't do much to influence
sales directly.'
'Good point.'
John went around the table, allowing each member of the team to give
their input. The consensus was that the targets were very ambitious;
probably too ambitious.

'What's the use of setting targets that are hopelessly unrealistic?' Bill asked. 'It's no good asking someone to run a marathon if they can't even run for a bus.'

Dietmar, who had been scribbling on a pad, started sketching on the flipchart (see Figure 8.3).

'I agree we have to set what we'd ideally like to achieve against what we are capable of. At the same time, we must be ambitious and push ourselves. I see it like this. If we aim too high and don't make it, then we capture the area bounded by these two dimensions: this tall, thin rectangle. But if we set objectives we can easily reach, like this long, flat rectangle, we don't benefit either. What he need to aim for is this.'

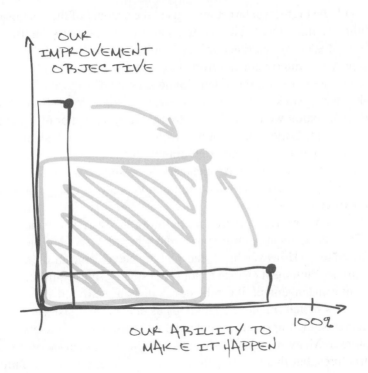

Figure 8.3 Capturing impact

Dietmar swapped the marker pen for a different colour and drew a squarer rectangle that was bigger than the others. 'To capture the biggest area of financial impact, we need to find a balance between our ambition and our capability to implement change.'

'I see what you mean,' said Brian. 'But what is our ability to implement?'

'We're about to find out,' said John.

Reconciling Business Need, Improvement Potential and Change Capability

Dietmar has hit on an important point. Too many operational transformations adopt the theoretical improvement potential identified in the diagnostic as the target for managers. This is a mistake for at least two reasons.

First, the diagnostic is looking for all sources of loss in the value chain and sets out to define perfection, so the scope for improvement is, in a sense, unbounded. In reality, capturing this potential is a long-term aspiration, not a one-off goal. In a culture of continuous improvement, managers set improvement targets each year so as gradually to close the gap with the ideal state.

Second, the high-level target must also take account of the organisation's capability to implement. Though this can't be measured scientifically, it can be evaluated by reference to qualitative criteria, such as the extent to which previous improvement efforts have fulfilled their objectives.

One company used a set of ten simple statements to evaluate its ability to make change stick (see Figure 8.4). Twenty people drawn from all levels of the organisation were asked how strongly they agreed or disagreed with each statement. Little more than a third felt the company had an effective approach to managing change programmes, or that previous initiatives had been successful. Among senior managers, the response was much the same. Not surprisingly, most respondents felt that the current change programme had a poor chance of success.

Holding up a mirror to the organisation in this way is a valuable exercise. The management team may not like what they see, but they need to acknowledge it. However bleak the picture may seem, an organisation's capability to implement change is not set in stone; with strong commitment from senior management, it can be developed and nurtured.

Dietmar's sketch (Figure 8.3) reminds us that a lean transformation fuses two elements: the improvement potential and the ability of the organisation to capture it. Many managers focus on changing the organisation's systems and structures, but this is only half the story. Plans are worthless until they have been implemented. The human aspects of the transformation, such as the motivation and engagement of the people involved, are just as important as the technical details.

When John visited Autoplast, he sensed an enthusiasm and engagement that he knows are lacking in his own workforce. He has begun to think about winning their hearts and minds – a challenge that will be just as crucial as designing a new layout for the assembly line or rethinking performance management systems.

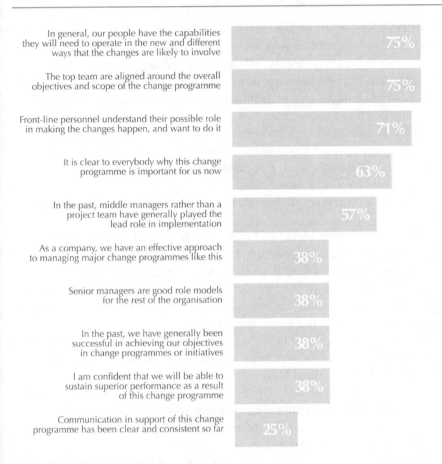

Figure 8.4 Evaluating change capability

The management team now embarks on a tour of the Bolton plant with Bruno and Dietmar.

The discussion about change capability had set everyone looking for clues. Dave explained they would visit the production area and the planning office to see the whole value stream.

In the assembly area, Bruno asked one of the operators, Mark Sherwell, what sort of things prevented him doing his job properly. Mark gestured at the gluing station.

'This old thing. It's forever breaking down. It's a nightmare.'

'What do you think we could do about it?' asked Bruno.

'I don't know,' Mark replied. 'Maybe buy a new machine that's more reliable?'

Bruno was worried, and not just because he knew Arboria couldn't afford to spend its way out of trouble. Mark seemed to lack the ability and the will to resolve his own problems, relying on technology instead. And if the machine was 'forever breaking down', what did that say about the relationship between production and maintenance? Why hadn't a recurring problem been fixed? Didn't maintenance have the resources or the know-how?

In the planning office, Christine explained how they scheduled production. They took consolidated orders from the sales database and entered the information manually into a separate scheduling system to generate a weekly build list for all departments.

'You have to retype all the information?' Bruno could hardly believe his ears.

'We know it's a problem,' Bill said. 'But the new IT system coming next year will allow the sales system to talk directly to the scheduling system.'

'And until then?' asked Bruno. 'Waiting for the new system isn't the answer. In any case, we're considering postponing that investment so we can concentrate on the lean transformation, especially if we can control production without relying so much on IT.'

They moved on to the mould shop, where Dietmar picked up the weekly schedule from one of the machines. Notes were scribbled all over it.

'What's this?' he asked Dave.

'Changes,' Dave replied. 'If the schedule changes for some reason, someone from planning comes down and marks up the schedule.'

'But why does the schedule change so much?'

'The customer,' Bill cut in.

'Surely it can't be just the customer if the orders are consolidated in advance and issued weekly?'

'It can. I wish it didn't happen that way, but it does.'

'I'd like to examine these changes in more detail if that's OK with you,' said Bruno.

Dave fetched Guy Lanbridge, the mould shop supervisor. He was obviously nervous, shifting from one foot to the other like a schoolboy in front of his head teacher. Dave explained they wanted to get a better understanding of scheduling changes by following an example through the process. He handed Guy the schedule.

'Now let me see . . . ah, yes, take that one,' Guy said. 'We had to stop the production run halfway through and change over to the toaster moulding, otherwise the assembly line would have run out of mouldings for the job they were putting together.'

'And that was because of an internal shortage of parts, rather than a customer change?' asked Dietmar.

'That's right.'

'And where are the parts stored?' asked Dietmar.

'In the warehouse.'

'Let's go and see.'

Guy showed them where the mouldings should have been.

'How come we didn't know we were short?' asked Dietmar.

There was an awkward silence. Guy looked at Dave.

'To be perfectly honest,' said Dave, 'we can't go by the stock data. People don't always book the parts out correctly if they're in a hurry, so we have to rely on knowing what we've got.'

'How do you do that? Do you keep all the parts for one product family together in one place?'

'We tried,' said Dave, 'but it just wasn't possible. It lasted a few weeks, but once the discipline went . . .'

'The diagnostic picked this up', said Philip. 'I don't know if you remember it from the MIFA? We talked about multiple stock locations for the same product code.'

'Yes, I remember,' said Bruno, shaking his head. The discussion was one thing; seeing the reality was another. If it hadn't been so worrying it might have been funny.

As they walked back to the meeting room for lunch, Bruno considered what to do. He felt like telling his management team that if they didn't buck their ideas up, he'd replace the lot of them. To be fair, though, they already knew about most of the problems from the diagnostic, as Philip had pointed out. He remembered Guy's anxiety at meeting the big boss, and knew what he had to do. The team had shared problems openly with him. If his response was to crush them, what kind of message would that send?

The visit brought home the value of spending time at the plant to see what was going on. Somehow management reports watered down the severity of the problems they were facing. He resolved to come back at regular intervals to judge for himself what impact the pilot was having.

Reconnecting Senior Managers with the Front Line

Bruno has discovered that experiencing issues at first hand makes them sink in much more deeply. He now has a feel for the challenge he faces in raising operational performance. The discussion with Mark Sherwell revealed that front-line people may be aware of problems, but do not take ownership of them. If a relatively simple piece of equipment is consistently unreliable, there must be a structural deficiency in the organisation: a failure of skills, of accountability, of systems, or maybe all three. Such underlying issues must be addressed before any permanent improvement can be achieved.

One of the reasons Bruno and Dietmar got such a lot out of their visit was that they asked probing questions to explore what was going on beneath the surface. Bruno could have gone further and used his encounters to indicate what he expects. When Mark suggested buying a new machine, Bruno's lack of response may have left him with the impression that his suggestion will be adopted. Instead, Bruno could have asked Mark what *we* could do to fix the problem.

The visit was also valuable in prompting Bruno to think about the effect his behaviour has on others. If he had criticised his management team, he would have taught them that exposing problems leads only to humiliation. Such acts can easily jeopardise lean programmes, which rely on revealing problems to stoke the improvement effort.

Consider scheduling changes. One way to ensure they don't disrupt production so often is to carry much higher stock levels. This will hide the problem, but not solve it. The lean process does the opposite; in effect, it says, 'Let's reduce the inventory level and see where it hurts first, then we'll be in a position to solve the problem.'

Instead of venting his frustration, Bruno asked the management team to draw up a plan to address the issues within four months, and pledged to return once every four weeks to review progress.

After the tour of the plant, the management team turned to organisation and people issues: the way performance should be managed on a daily basis and over the long term; how the organisation structure should reflect operational changes; what training managers and those working in the pilot area might need; and the alignment of performance indicators and reporting processes with new flows and processes. Take the mould shop: it currently focuses on production output, but soon it will be expected to manage the level of inventory downstream too, so its performance indicators will need adjustment.

Louise emphasized the need to link people development processes with the overall improvement effort. She'd been trying for some time to get managers to take personal appraisals more seriously, but most still treated them as a box-ticking exercise. Here was an opportunity to do away with much of the formal evaluation process and rely instead on the daily cycle of team-based problem solving and performance monitoring.

After the workshop, John asked Philip to take the lead in drawing up plans to implement the future state in the coffee maker product family. A few days later, having drafted a proposal, Philip goes to see John.

'I think it makes sense to divide the work up into three main areas: upstream, assembly and organisation.'

'OK. Go on.'

'Upstream would look at the mould shop and focus first on improving reliability to free up capacity, and then on speeding up changeovers to create flexibility. Assembly includes creating standards, balancing the line to *Takt* for different levels of demand, and changing its layout to improve flow and productivity. I've lumped everything else into organisation: performance monitoring, tracking and resolving production problems, team structure, and suchlike.'

'What about planning? I thought we'd be making big changes to the way we schedule production.'

'Absolutely. The point where the customer order enters the production process will be at the assembly stage, so I've included it in the assembly work stream. I thought about treating it separately, but then we risk not ending up with an integrated solution.'

'That sounds right. But what about scheduling moulding?' John asked.

'Their production requirement will effectively be determined by the downstream process – that's assembly. We might need to make an exception for when we build ahead at the peak season, but we'll cross that bridge when we come to it.'

'Isn't that a bit risky? Do you have a plan in mind?'

'To some extent, it depends how successful we are in the mould shop. The more capacity we can release by eliminating losses, the less we'll need to build ahead.'

'Well, Phil, you can imagine what a difference that would make to the business,' John said with feeling. 'But what about the resources? Who's going to do all this work?'

'I think each work stream should be led by a member of the management team to make sure it has enough weight behind it. I had Dave in mind for the assembly work stream. For the upstream one, where the activities are focused on equipment, I thought Trevor Radcliffe, as maintenance manager, would be the best bet.'

'And the organisation work?'

'What about you?'

'Hmm. I'm not sure,' John replied, leaning back in his swivel chair and turning to look out of the window. He thought for a moment and turned back to face Philip.

'I could do it, but I wonder whether you shouldn't take the lead, Phil. You're new to the organisation, so you've got a fresh perspective, and you've got experience of other ways of doing things. I reckon you're more likely to get honest opinions about what needs fixing than I am. That's not the sort of question people like the boss asking them!'

The suggestion took Philip by surprise, but it made sense. It also felt like a vote of confidence.

'OK. I'd be happy to lead that work. But I still think it'll require close involvement from you.'

'You can count on me for that.'

As Philip turned to leave, John called him back.

'Phil, there is one thing that's bothering me.'

'Yes?'

'It's Bill. I notice he doesn't have a leadership role in this.'

'That's true. Do you think we should . . .?'

'No. I've been watching him over the last few weeks. To be honest, I'm starting to wonder if he's going to be able to make this change.'

'Have you spoken to him?'

'Not yet. It's awkward; we go back a long way. But leave it with me. I'll talk to him.'

'If it's any consolation, John, it's normal in my experience for a few people not to be able to change their way of working. In the long run, it's better for them and us that they move on. You may find Bill is having doubts too, and would welcome a chance to discuss them.'

'You could be right. We'll see. Thanks, Phil. Great work, by the way.'

Having had his plans approved in principle by John, Philip went to see Donkey Dave and Trevor Radcliffe to bring them up to date and share his thoughts about what the pilot might mean for them. He explained that the objectives of the implementation would be closely aligned with their normal responsibilities, and the experience they gained would stand them in good stead in their future roles.

Philip then set out the plan for each work stream in the form of a Gantt chart showing the main activities for the next four months, their sequence, objectives, and the people responsible. One objective was to reduce changeover times in the mould shop to less than 30 minutes by the end of the four-month pilot.

Louise worked with Philip to develop a communication plan to launch the change effort and keep everyone informed about progress. Together, they undertook a stakeholder analysis to identify key stakeholders and their likely concerns so as to ensure that communications were appropriately targeted in format as well as content. Louise suggested that Dave should play a lead role in communicating to workers on the shop floor because of his skill with people and his personal credibility.

Things were falling into place. As the management team finalised the plans for the pilot, anticipation grew among the people at the plant.

Communicating to the Wider Organisation

In preparing the communication plan, Louise and Philip conducted a stakeholder analysis: a method of identifying the main people involved in a change programme and grouping them by their particular interests so that key messages can be delivered through appropriate channels, whether it be newsletters, videos or face-to-face briefings by managers. Stakeholder analysis can also be used to define meaningful roles for the key 'influencers' in the organisation: those people whose formal roles and position give them power or whose knowledge and relationships give them influence.

The analysis also offers an opportunity to consider what to do with people who may be unable or unwilling to accept change. Bill has shown on several occasions that he isn't behind the effort. At the moment, he wields a certain amount of power within the organisation; he may fear he'll be marginalised by a more transparent method of scheduling production, or that it will call into question his effectiveness as a manager. As a senior figure at the plant, he could prove disruptive to the change programme if his opposition isn't handled appropriately. Such people often need to be moved away from the change activity.

Managers sometimes shy away from these tough decisions until it's too late, but ducking the issue benefits no one. When a multinational packaging manufacturer introduced a lean improvement programme, its results in North America far exceeded those in Europe. One of the reasons was that the American CEO replaced half his management team within a year, whereas the European leaders made much less drastic changes. Replacing managers who can't or won't effect change sends a powerful signal to the rest of the organisation that top management is serious about carrying out its intentions.

All too often, senior managers take communication to mean sharing their perspectives with subordinates, but this is strictly a one-way process. To be effective, communication must be a two-way dialogue. It must also be couched in the language of those involved. Bruno may be motivated by an ROCE of 16 per cent, but the people who assemble coffee makers will want to know whether they have to work faster or continue to put up with unreliable machines. The communication challenge is to address these questions as well as conveying the positive effects of lean.

Part of the difficulty is that front-line people in many organisations are so used to hearing the same messages at the start of every new change programme that they've grown deaf to what they see as empty promises. Something distinctive and compelling will be needed to get through this initiative fatigue. Though people are inclined to ignore what they regard as propaganda, they are usually engaged by a good story which connects at an emotional level, drawing people into the experience so that they care about what happens next.

When planning change communications, managers should ask: what is our change story? Why should our staff care? What can they identify with? A good change story describes a company's past, present and future in a way that the audience will find exciting and easy to understand. It must explain why change is not just necessary, but urgent – perhaps by spelling out what will happen if the company does nothing to address the challenges it faces. For Arboria UK, the compelling need to change is to reverse the long-term decline in order to secure its future.

Having established the need for change, the story then needs to paint an appealing picture of the future and show how the organisation gets from here to there. The account of this journey shouldn't be confined to the route but should touch on the way people behave in the new scheme of things. To engage people's enthusiasm, the story must be capable of being retold and personalised by everyone in the organisation, though it should be owned and developed by the senior team, particularly the CEO and change leaders. A story emanating from the CEO will be seen as having greater validity and authenticity. It follows that the best way to hear the story is from the horse's mouth: ideally the CEO, or failing that, another leader.

Once a story has been brought to life, it can be reinforced in a combination of ways: a memo or e-mail from the CEO to all employees, a video, a road show that travels to each site, or a booklet. The key is to choose a vehicle that's appropriate to the audience, and to give the audience opportunities to digest the story and react to it through workshops, conversations, or formal group or individual discussions.

A change story that is repeated and reinterpreted over time comes to form a common thread of imagery running through the whole organisation. The CEO of a retail chain might construct a story around an encounter he or she had with a customer and what it taught him or her about the need for change. Stories are more likely to take on a life of their own if they are vivid and concrete and involve anecdotes about individuals, rather than being conceptual or impersonal.

As the old saw suggests, actions speak louder than words, so to be truly convincing a change story must be reinforced by practical and persuasive demonstrations that show the impact of the new way of working.

In the next chapter, we follow the team at Arboria as they begin to implement the plans they have made.

CHAPTER 9

Demonstrating the Change

- The pilot must demonstrate the benefits of lean not just for the business, but also for employees.
- The pilot will uncover systems-level issues that managers need to address to ensure sustainability.
- The implementation of the future state must be driven by line managers, not a project team.

The next phase of Arboria's journey to lean is to carry out the pilot. A successful implementation will both achieve the planned business objectives and demonstrate the benefits of the new way of working to front-line personnel, who may need convincing that it can produce real improvements in their working lives. The pilot also affords an opportunity to pressure-test the organisation and its management infrastructure to identify weak spots that must be addressed if change is to be sustained over time.

Although a small team led by Philip will support the pilot implementation at Arboria, it is line managers who need to take the lead in driving the change. Senior managers should be involved in regular progress reviews, improvement activities and workshops. They need to work alongside front-line personnel to understand the issues as well as engage in problem solving. By taking part, senior managers demonstrate their commitment to the effort and can see for themselves whether improvements are taking hold.

We rejoin the Arboria team as they start to explain the reasons for the lean transformation to everyone at the plant.

The management team have been debating the best way to launch the pilot. At first, John was keen to get everyone together during the shift handover one Friday morning, but Dave felt such a 'big bang' launch would only fuel people's cynicism, and suggested John hold a smaller meeting to brief department managers instead. These managers could then brief their direct reports who would in turn brief front-line teams. Louise agreed, saying that line managers would be able to explain lean in their own words and tie its objectives into the agendas for their own departments, so making the effort more relevant.

Building on what she'd done with Philip after the management team workshop, Louise worked with John on the communications. They used Dave as a sounding board. He soon raised the question of redundancies.

'It's on everyone's mind. After all, every other initiative has involved people being laid off.'

'We can't talk about redundancies at the kick-off,' John snapped. 'It'll get people's backs up before we even start.'

'But if we don't tackle it, people will think we've got something to hide.'

'What do you suggest?'

'Tell them the truth.'

'The truth is, I don't know if there will be redundancies or not. It'll depend on whether we can grow sales fast enough to absorb the productivity improvements.'

'Say that then. People aren't daft. They understand business realities and they'll appreciate honesty. It's got to be better than saying nothing. We can't ask managers and team leaders to speak to their people and then not give them answers to difficult questions.'

'I suppose you're right. OK, let's include it.'

So Louise worked with Dave to prepare some of these answers. She also spent a couple of hours training managers on how to run the briefings so that they would naturally lead into a discussion. The preparation paid off during the communication cascade over the following week. John's personal commitment came through in his blunt style, and some of his enthusiasm rubbed off on the department managers, who made a reasonable job of engaging their teams.

That Friday, nearly a fortnight after the management workshop with Bruno, Philip called his team together to confirm the plans for the following week. The original diagnostic team had been augmented by Donkey Dave and Trevor Radcliffe. Dave would lead the assembly work stream with help from Fiona Richardson, the team leader, and Steve Edwards, the production engineer. In the upstream work, Trevor would be supported by Steve's colleague Lisa Hallum and Derek Hines, the maintenance engineer. Guy Lanbridge, the mould shop supervisor, would take the lead in implementing changes, and Christine McGuire would provide support on issues related to production planning.

Philip explained that he planned to devote most of his time to coaching these teams until they were up and running. He also intended to work closely with Louise and Brian to develop the right organisation structure and performance management systems to support the new ways of working.

'As we move towards the future-state operating system, it can help to think of four phases: stability, flow, *Takt* and pull. First we need to stabilise the process, then we need to create continuous flow wherever we can. It's vital in the assembly area, but it also applies to the links between the mould shop and assembly, and between assembly and the finished goods stock. Once we have established flow, we'll balance the line to the *Takt* time so that we make coffee makers at the rate the customer requires them. Finally, we'll implement a pull system to control production.'

'What do you mean by stabilising production?' Steve asked.

'It's like putting down a foundation before you build a house. In the timing plan, we've devoted a few weeks to things like creating standards, documenting skill levels, analysing machine breakdowns and that kind of thing. It may not be exciting, but it's a great way to get to know the process and the people, and we have to do it before we can implement the new operating system. For example, we can't reduce our finished goods stock until we have a reliable process upstream, otherwise we risk being caught out if a machine goes down.'

'And what's "implementing performance monitoring"?' asked Derek, pointing to the plan on the training room wall.

'That's an important part of establishing stability,' Philip replied. 'We need to track how much the process produces on an hourly basis from week one, and use this information to manage performance and understand the level of variability.'

'And what about "implement problem resolution"?' Derek continued, reading the next item from the plan.

'In a way, that's the second half of performance monitoring. You know the PDCA cycle: plan, do, check, act? Well, performance monitoring allows us to check production against the plan, but we also need a mechanism for resolving any problems that get in the way.'

He picked up a pen and sketched on the whiteboard. 'The problem resolution system is basically a simple document that's posted in the production area. It has three columns beginning with 'c': concern, cause and countermeasure. At the end of each shift, team leaders record any problems that occurred that day in the concern column. If they can, they also fill in the cause and countermeasure columns, but they may need help from other people to understood the root cause and work out how to fix it.'

'Sounds OK,' said Guy.

'Yes, but it sounds easier than it is,' Philip warned. 'These systems just become wallpaper if they aren't used every day. That's why we'll introduce them just in the pilot area initially, rather than across the whole site. We shouldn't set things up unless we're committed to seeing them through.' He paused. 'Nothing will discredit our work faster than if we make promises we don't keep.'

Creating a Stable Platform

Now that everyone in the organisation knows about the lean transformation, expectations have been raised, and it will be all too easy for the Arboria team to become preoccupied with delivering change quickly. Philip reminds them that the early weeks of implementation are about establishing a foundation for what's to follow. The journey to lean is a marathon, not a sprint. That doesn't mean people should reject opportunities to capture quick wins, but they must stay the course and stick to the plan.

Stability is a prerequisite. The new operating system will be impossible to implement if variations in materials, equipment performance and skills and working methods prevent a reliable product flow from being established. Unless Arboria can improve the reliability of its gluing station, it won't be able to create a continuous flow of parts in the assembly area – or convince people that lean can make a real difference to their working conditions.

Clear operating standards must be devised to ensure that tasks are carried out consistently and safely. They should include the standard time taken for each task. This information acts as a basis for allocating work content correctly at different *Takt* times, and for making improvements to the process to reduce the overall work content.

Stability in the operating system requires discipline in mindsets and behaviour. If the team leader doesn't have the discipline to hold a five-minute review at the end of each shift to record problems that have occurred and check that countermeasures have worked, stability won't improve.

As the teams implement performance monitoring on the assembly line and in the mould shop, we'll see that an apparently simple change makes considerable demands on the team leaders.

At eight o'clock the following Monday, it was time to brief the production teams, explain the implementation plans in more detail and outline the main activities for the week ahead.

Lisa had produced a log sheet for the mould shop operators to complete; it would record all losses from breakdowns, changeovers, minor stops and defective parts. The team would use the information to calculate the overall equipment effectiveness (OEE) of each machine so that they could target improvement activities appropriately. Once this was done, Christine would consider how products could be dedicated to the machines in line with the capacity available. Lisa had asked Guy to explain the log sheet to the mould shop team during his shop floor briefing.

'Lisa's prepared a log sheet that she'd like you all to fill in,' Guy said, handing everyone a copy. 'I think it's pretty self-explanatory. Any questions?'

'Actually, yes,' said Howard Ashworth, a stocky man in his fifties, waving the page at Lisa. 'Why do we need to fill in another sheet when we already have the shift report? Can't you get the information off that?'

'He's right,' a colleague added. 'You're just asking us to do the same work twice. I thought this project was about doing things more efficiently.'

'It is, but the shift reports don't give us the information we need,' Lisa replied, hoping Guy would back her up. He didn't.

'Well, which one should we use, Lisa?' asked Guy.

She hesitated.

'Look, we've got parts to make,' said Howard, looking at his watch. 'Why don't you get your act together, then we can talk about which piece of paper you want us to fill in.' He handed the log sheet back to Lisa and walked away. The briefing was over.

This wasn't how Lisa had planned it. She felt Guy had let her down. When he'd agreed to explain the new procedure to his team, she'd expected some support. But he'd made her look green and naive. She decided to seek Trevor's advice.

Over on the assembly line, things had got off to a better start. Fiona ran through the performance monitoring board prepared by Steve. It was a dry-wipe board with a row for each hour and columns for production target, actual number produced, and cumulative production against the target. There was also a column for noting any problems that occurred during the hour and an estimate of the time that had been lost. She asked the person packing coffee makers to fill in the board every hour and be sure to write down any problems, however trivial.

Dave explained that they would use the information to draw up a list of the problems that needed to be resolved to help the assembly team be more productive. He also told them that Steve would begin creating visual standards during the week.

'But we've been doing the job for years. Why do we need to write it down all of a sudden?' asked Eileen Mayoh, one of the operators.

'We need to agree the best way of doing things so we know how long each step takes when we start rejigging the workload to meet different levels of demand.'

'You're not going to get your watch out again, are you, Steve?' she teased.

'Afraid so,' he replied. 'During the diagnostic, we wanted to find out roughly how much work there was at each station, but now we want to see how long each job should take when there aren't any problems.'

'But there always are. That's what you don't seem to understand. Of course we could work faster if things didn't go wrong, but they do.'

'Eileen's got a point', said Fiona. 'It might be an idea for you to work on the line for a day, to get a feel for the things that do go wrong. How about it, Steve? Dave?'

'It's a great idea,' said Dave. 'It'll do you good to do some real work for a change!'

'I'm game,' Steve agreed.

'Great. Eileen, will you look after Steve and get him started?'

'Don't worry, Fiona, he'll be safe with us.' Eileen grinned.

Steve worked on the line for the whole day. Everyone else was experienced and made the work look easy. He could just about keep up until he hit a snag, and then it all fell apart. The unreliable gluing machine was particularly annoying; no wonder the team kept on about it.

'We've been telling them about these things for years,' the operator, Mark Sherwell, said bitterly. 'That gluing machine for instance: we've been promised by every man and his dog that it'll be sorted out, but it's still a pile of crap. We'd be better off with a pot of glue and a brush!'

Steve's day on the line gave him a useful insight into people's concerns. The biggest was redundancy. Eileen had been with the company for almost

20 years, and had seen many friends asked to leave. She feared that by improving the process, she and the others would be doing themselves out of a job. Steve tried to persuade her that making the business more secure would benefit everyone in the end, but he could see she wasn't convinced.

Working with the team also gave Steve a good grounding for creating the standards. Fiona did most of the timing, which prevented any repeat of the awkward incident that had occurred during the diagnostic.

Though the team grumbled about filling in the performance monitoring board every hour, saying it disrupted their work, they got on with it all the same. Philip and Dave both made a point of looking at the board whenever they were passing. In fact, the effect on production was immediate: the team began to hit or exceed every target – a distinct improvement on past performance.

In the second week of implementation, Steve had a simple fixture made for the assembly line to ease a fiddly job he'd struggled with during his day on the line. He then retimed the job and updated the standard. Since this station was a bottleneck, he also raised the hourly targets on the performance monitoring board to take account of the improvement.

Next day, the team fell behind. Fiona noticed and checked the board: no problems. But when she approached the team, they accused her and the others of using the board to pressurise them into working harder. Fiona felt torn between them and Steve, who she could see had sound reasons for increasing the target. She realised she should discuss the performance gap with her team, but couldn't imagine how to do it without being confrontational. Having always got results by being one of the gang, she feared that setting herself apart as a manager would damage her good working relationship with her team.

Establishing a Performance Culture

We learn a lot about the team leaders, Fiona and Guy, from the way they handle the changes in their areas.

When Lisa introduces the new log sheet to the mould shop production team, she receives hardly any support from Guy, the line manager. By querying its purpose, Howard is implicitly challenging the authority of its originator. Guy fails to take ownership and effectively hands the challenge over to Lisa, who lacks the status and credibility to resist it.

In the early stages of implementation, team leaders are often asked to manage their teams, perhaps for the first time. They may feel out of their depth, or be unwilling to take on the responsibility. One food manufacturer undertaking a lean transformation discovered that most of its team leaders were more interested in taking early redundancy than in stepping up to the role of managing performance.

It's vital to involve people in shaping a desired outcome; telling them what to do isn't enough. Howard has spent his life working with injection-moulding machines. He's unlikely to change the way he works just because a young production engineer comes along with a document that he sees no need for. Lisa could have involved Howard and his colleagues in designing the log sheet and rationalising existing paperwork.

When Steve improved a process and then raised the production target, the team saw it as a trick to make them work harder. Although people claim that lean is about working smarter, not harder, the truth is that removing waste from the process does often make people feel they are working harder because they spend less time on waiting and other activities that add little or no value. Fiona fears that supporting the changes will jeopardise her good-natured working relationships, but she will face similar challenges in the future, and needs to decide whether she is willing to tackle them and how she can take her team with her. One obvious means is to show them that the lean transformation will do away with some of their problems.

It came as no surprise that one problem dominated the performance monitoring board: the gluing machine. It failed so often in the first few days that Jeff just wrote 'FIX THE GLUING MACHINE' across the board and left it at that. It was the first item that Fiona wrote up on the new problem resolution sheet, and took on symbolic weight as a test case for the lean implementation team's promise to address the sources of loss.

After a short debate about who should take the lead in resolving the problem, Steve's name was written on the board. He cast his mind back to a training course he'd attended a few months before. As he remembered, the first step in solving a problem was to define it, and the second was to observe it closely and gather data. Defining the problem was easy enough: the pneumatically operated cylinders often stuck in position. He'd already kept a note of how often the machine jammed and tried to investigate possible causes when he was drafting the standards.

The third step was to use such tools as the fishbone diagram and the 'five whys' to arrive at a hypothesis of what might be causing the problem. The fourth step was to act on this by making appropriate changes. The fifth and sixth steps were to study the results and standardise the new condition.

To find out the cause, Steve set up a meeting with Eileen from the assembly line and a maintenance technician well versed in pneumatics. At the technician's suggestion, he also called in an engineer from P. J. Tippins, the local company that had supplied the machine. The cause turned out to be remarkably simple. The technician found that one of the shafts was scored and slightly bent, probably because someone had had a go at it with a hammer. In addition, the engineer from Tippins discovered that the lubricant used on the machine was attacking the seals, causing the pressure to drop. It looked as though these two factors, combined with the glue splattered liberally over the workings, were making the machine jam.

Any embarrassment Steve felt at the ease of identifying the causes soon faded when the problem cleared up. To prevent it recurring, he asked Tippins to draft a simple maintenance standard for the people who used the machine on a daily basis. All in all, this was a great demonstration of the practical benefits of lean for people working on the line.

As Eileen put it, 'We've been complaining about that machine forever and a day. I wish somebody had done something about it before, but better late than never!'

This early success boosted the assembly team's production output as well as their morale. Now that one of the biggest sources of instability had been eliminated, Steve and Fiona could start to improve the material flow by rebalancing the workload, removing unnecessary work in progress and reconfiguring the layout of the line.

Back at the mould shop, progress was slower. Lisa felt they had taken one step forward and two steps back when they introduced the new log sheet, but they had agreed they had to do whatever was necessary to get it right.

'If you don't take them with you on this, you'll never get them back', Dave said. He offered to support Lisa and Guy in working with the team to find a solution that everyone could agree. Next day, Lisa and Dave attended the meeting that Guy now held at the start of every shift. Once Guy had run through the priorities for each machine and the changeovers for the shift, Dave took over.

'I know there's been a few words about the new log sheet that Lisa prepared, and I want to add my bit. According to the numbers, we're running the machines at around 100 per cent utilisation, sometimes more, but we all know it's not like that: machines suffer from breakdowns, changeovers take hours, and parts aren't always up to scratch. I might not be the sharpest tool in the box but even I can work out that something must be wrong somewhere; we can't be working at 100 per cent and have all this downtime. It doesn't add up.

'That's why we have to find a better way of measuring the performance of the machines so we know where the problems are and what the prize will be if we can fix them. I'm sure you've all seen what's happened to the gluing machine on the assembly line. A mould machine might be more complex, but the challenge needs to be tackled in exactly the same way.

'So, the bottom line is that changing our performance measures isn't negotiable, but the way we do it is. I've asked Lisa to work with you to put together a log sheet that everyone can cope with. If there are any problems, Guy and I are here to listen. Now is everyone OK with that?'

Dave didn't expect a response. He would follow up with Howard in private after the meeting. He'd made it clear that the team couldn't choose who they worked with; Lisa would see the log sheet through no matter what.

Tackling Deep-Seated Problems

Fixing the gluing machine was a milestone in Arboria's lean journey: the first material improvement for people at the front line. Let's examine what it took to plug this long-standing leak in the value stream.

First, the problem was made visible to management. Once Bruno knew about it, it could no longer be hidden, and it became a management rather than shop floor problem. Second, someone – Steve – was made accountable for fixing it. Third, a structured approach was adopted to get to the root cause and put the problem right. Fourth, a team of people with the necessary knowledge and skills was brought together to solve the problem.

The lack of standards for maintaining the gluing machine suggested a lack of attention to detail and a lack of accountability for maintenance, so that minor problems fell between the responsibilities of maintenance, engineering and production. Although this clearly reveals a deficit within the operating system, raising and maintaining the performance of the machine will also require the right management infrastructure and mindsets and behaviour.

As the team continued to work on the pilot implementation, John assessed their progress through weekly reviews.

Philip, Dave and Trevor held an hour-long review with John at three o'clock every Friday to review the week's activities against the implementation plan.

Before the meeting, Philip put together a one-page report with graphs covering four performance indicators: overall equipment effectiveness (OEE), average changeover time on the mould machines, labour productivity on the assembly line and overall lead time. The report summarised the activities completed that week, such as 'visual standards completed on assembly line' and 'machine breakdown data analysed to identify priorities', and set out activities for the following week. There was also a list of issues needing John's attention, such as the approval of purchase orders.

This report formed the basis for the entire meeting. Rather than generating extra material, they used real documents, such as the visual standards Steve had drawn up with Fiona and the team, so as to reflect what was happening in the pilot as directly as possible. They also held the meeting in the training room rather than John's office, and walked through the factory just before or after it to look at recent changes. By talking to production operators about the pilot, John was able to bring himself up to speed and demonstrate his ongoing commitment to the workforce.

During the third weekly review, the group discussed the successful resolution of the problem with the gluing machine, which John had seen just before the meeting. Philip took the opportunity to question the way they approached basic maintenance tasks.

'We've got to ask why it took so long to fix such a persistent problem. To my mind it's a symptom of a wider issue, which is the way production and maintenance work together.'

'Go on,' said John.

'Well, production reported the problem again and again until they gave up and took matters into their own hands, which could be how the shaft got damaged in the first place.'

'How can that happen, Trevor? How does it slip through the net?'

'It's not so much that it slips through the net, John, it's more that the net is full to bursting. We have to prioritise, and of course we put the mould machines first.'

'Which is the right thing to do from a business perspective,' added Philip.

'But it frustrates the hell out of assembly,' said John.

'Exactly!' said Philip.

'And what about the mould shop?' asked John. 'Do they get the service they need?'

Dave spoke up. 'I would say no, they don't. As Trevor says, if there's a backlog there's always going to be compromises. I'm sure Trevor would agree we're not on top of it.'

'Too true. We've got a programme of preventive maintenance on the mould machines, but we're always chasing our tails to clear the breakdowns, so things get put off and we quickly get into a vicious cycle.'

'What do you suggest, Phil?' asked John.

'We've discussed a few ideas. It's still early days as yet, but broadly what we're suggesting is that we should split the maintenance department in two. One part would be dedicated to supporting production; it would report to the production supervisors and then on to Dave. The other part

would focus on highly skilled technical work and the preventive maintenance programme. That way we could ring-fence preventive maintenance
to stop it being pulled apart by day-to-day problems, and give production a
dedicated resource it can manage according to its own priorities.'

'I can see the logic. What do you think, Trevor? Will it fly with your lads?'

'It won't be easy; I can think of conversations I'd rather have. But we've
talked it through and I can't see a better way.'

'OK. Let's discuss it at the plant management meeting next week. Could
you pull together a proposal before then?'

'Sure,' said Philip.

The following week Bruno and Dietmar made the first of their promised
monthly visits. Philip had prepared a short status review based on the last
weekly report, and took them through it, explaining that the main theme of
the first month had been to establish a platform of stability. Dave and
Trevor went through the practical details of establishing systems for
performance monitoring and problem resolution. This took about half an
hour. Then the meeting moved into the factory so that Bruno and Dietmar
could see what progress had been made since their last visit.

The tour began on the assembly line. Before Fiona could show them the
standards that had been developed for each workstation, Bruno noticed the
gluing machine.

'It looks much better!' he remarked to no one in particular.

Steve ushered Eileen over to explain how they had solved the problem.
Her enthusiasm couldn't have been further from Mark Sherwell's negative
attitude of just a month earlier. Now, however, Mark was also very positive
about the improvement. Bruno was delighted, and Philip had to drag him
away when it was time to move on to the mould shop.

Lisa had spent a lot of time with Guy and Howard to come up with a
simpler log sheet and help them prepare for this visit. Guy introduced
everyone to Howard, who picked up the clipboard hanging on his machine
and showed them the sheet he'd been filling in since his shift began.

'The log sheet is like a truck's tachometer: it tells us exactly what the
machine has been doing throughout the shift. We write down how many
parts we make and record the cycle time. This gives us all the information
we need to work out how many parts we should have produced in the shift.
Here, we note down all the stoppages. If it's a breakdown, we record when
the machine stopped and when we got it back up and running. If it's a
minor stop – a part getting stuck in the mould or something – we just tick
one of these categories. We also log any quality defects, whether we find
them here or assembly pick them up, and knock them off the total.'

'And what about changeovers?' asked Dietmar.

'Oh, yes. We had quite a ding-dong about how to record them,' said Howard, looking at Lisa. 'But Lisa twisted my arm and I agreed we should count the time from the last good part produced with the old tool to the first good part produced with the new tool.'

'If we hadn't,' said Lisa, 'we'd be improving just one small part of the thing and might be missing important stuff like the material changeover or preparing the new tool.'

'Sounds like a great piece of work,' said Dietmar. 'Can I have a copy of the log sheet?'

Keeping Senior Managers Involved

During implementation, the usual role of senior managers is to review progress against the plan to ensure that the pilot demonstrates the benefits of the future state. But they also need to get directly involved in implementation so that the pilot can fulfil its second key objective: to uncover the systems-level issues that managers must address before change can be sustained over the long term.

While John takes part in weekly progress reviews, Bruno and Dietmar stay in touch through monthly visits. For all of them, the priority is to see for themselves what is going on, not have it summed up in some formal report or presentation. Such first-hand experience is critical if they are to distil the lessons from the pilot when they implement lean across the rest of the operation.

In the hour or so Bruno spends on the shop floor, his behaviour differs noticeably from that of his previous visit. He seems more at home on the shop floor, probably because he now has his own reference points and contacts. When he goes to the assembly line, he checks on the state of the gluing machine: a rare opportunity to circumvent the reporting structure and see for himself the impact lean is having at the plant.

Executives are fed a staple diet of statistics and balanced scorecards, but many love incidents and anecdotes and use them to great effect in engaging others. Bruno is no exception. He's bound to share his experiences with ExCo and the other plant managers as he builds support and momentum for the lean transformation.

The pilot team have done a lot of groundwork to establish the stability needed to improve the flow of material through the value stream without compromising customer service. But the rest of the business is still plagued by instability and changing priorities.

John put down the phone and got up to open a window. He was feeling hot all of a sudden. The call had been from Homestar, one of Arboria's top three customers, asking where its delivery was. This was the second missed delivery this month, which was why the purchasing director had called him direct. Homestar was a big pan-European retailer, and this was a relationship John couldn't afford to jeopardise. He'd promised to check out the missed delivery himself and call back that afternoon. He picked up the phone and dialled Dave's number.

For the past few weeks, Philip had taken more of a back seat, coaching and guiding the team as they worked to the pilot plans. He was now thinking about implementing lean across the whole site. He'd spent the morning roughing out ideas on timing, sequence and resources. After lunch, he decided to take a walk through the plant.

At the assembly line, Philip was surprised to see that the performance monitoring board hadn't been filled in that morning and the operators were packing up even though the end of their shift was still 20 minutes away. He spoke to Mark.

'Hi, Mark. Is Fiona about?'

'No. I haven't seen her for a while. Last time I did she was heading for the mould shop to chase mouldings.'

'Surely we haven't run out?'

'Afraid so, just in the last couple of hours. We were able to build until about midday, but there's been a problem with raw material or something.'

'Raw material? That's odd. I'll check.' Before he left, Philip pointed to the blank performance monitoring board. 'Why hasn't this been completed today?'

'Sorry, Philip, we've been run off our feet. What with one thing and another, it didn't get done. I'll make sure we're back on track tomorrow.'

'So has everything been OK apart from the mouldings?'

'Yeah.' Mark paused to think. 'We've had nothing major, have we, Eileen?'

'Just little things.'

'Like what?' Philip asked.

'Oh, the gluing machine's playing up a bit. Nothing like as bad as before, but it's tripped out a few times for some reason.'

'So what did you do?' Philip enquired.

'We just reset it.'

'Did that solve the problem?'

'Not exactly, but it kept us going.' Eileen held up her hands. 'I know what you're going to say. We should get to the root cause and sort it out, but it's just been one of those days.'

'I know that, Eileen, but days like today will happen from time to time, and if we don't learn from them they'll happen again and again until we're back where we started. If we don't keep up the performance monitoring board and record all the issues, they'll never make it onto the radar screen. Think about the gluing machine: getting it on the agenda was half the battle.'

'You're right,' Mark sighed, 'but it's so easy to take your eye off the ball.'

'Yes, but it's up to you as a team to keep us honest. It's all about maintaining these basic disciplines. If you stop raising the issues, the people you depend on to support you – managers, maintenance, whoever – will think everything is fine and spend their time on something else instead.'

Aware that the shift was almost over and he had made his point, Philip let them go. At the gluing machine, he opened the maintenance file Steve had set up. If the record sheets were accurate, daily checks hadn't been completed for the past few days; nor had the first monthly preventive maintenance taken place. Here was confirmation of his suspicion that basic disciplines were slipping.

Instead of going to the mould shop to check out the raw materials supply himself, Philip decided to consult Dave. He paged him from the nearest phone. A few seconds later, it rang back.

'Hi, Dave, it's Philip. Thanks for calling back. I could do with a quick chat. Where are you?'

'In the warehouse and up to my neck in it.'

'What's up?'

'John's doing his nut because of another missed delivery to Homestar, and half the mould shop are sitting on their backsides because of crap raw material.'

'What's wrong with it?'

'Some bright spark in Brussels has centralised all our contracts to cut costs, so we've switched suppliers. The specification is meant to be the same, but the bloody machines don't seem to know that.'

'Obviously this isn't a good time to talk. I'll let you get on and catch up with you tomorrow.'

Next day, Philip raised his concerns about the implementation with John. He described what he'd seen and heard on the assembly line and suggested that the management team get together to discuss the situation.

'I hear what you're saying, Phil, but there's no way we can spare the time at the moment.'

'We can't just let this go or we'll be resigning ourselves to being bounced around by every little incident. If we're serious about lean, we have to commit to making it happen.'

'Tell you what, let's discuss it at the next review meeting on Friday.'

'We'll need more time than that, John. This won't be a five-minute discussion.'

'All right, let's do it afterwards then.' John glanced at his diary. 'Oh no, I'm in Brussels on Friday. Dietmar rang this morning and asked me to go over to discuss the ramp-up plan for new products. You'll have to go ahead without me.'

'I'm not prepared to do that, John', said Philip. 'Either we do this properly, or not at all.'

There was an awkward silence.

'OK,' John said finally. 'I'll call Dietmar and see if we can do it by phone. If not, we'll just have to find a time next week when we can all get together.'

In the event, John managed to put his meeting with Dietmar back to the following week, so the management team got together on Friday afternoon at the end of the review meeting to discuss the problems. Philip shared his concern at the loss of focus on the part of the management team, who were leaving it all to the pilot implementation team.

Dave admitted he'd spent less time on the pilot than he would have liked; the raw material fiasco had got in the way. Trevor promised to look into the failure to carry out preventive maintenance on the gluing machine, but explained they were short-staffed as another firm had poached one of his best technicians.

At this point, John's mobile rang and he left the room. True to form, Bill took the opportunity to say he'd always had doubts about the new approach. They were still arguing 15 minutes later when John returned.

'How's it going?' he asked. 'All sorted?'

There was an uncomfortable silence before Philip spoke. 'What we have to ask ourselves is whether these issues are just a bump in the road that we'll soon get over, or something more serious.'

John suggested they go round the table so that everyone could air any issues that were preventing them giving their full support to the pilot. When pushed, Trevor admitted he could do with extra resources, and suggested borrowing an apprentice from the tool room for a few weeks to clear the maintenance backlog. Dave said he could use some support from John to sort out raw materials. Trying to resolve a Brussels issue locally was taking a lot of his time.

By the end of the meeting, everyone had acknowledged they would have to do things differently to keep the implementation on track. As the meeting broke up, Philip spoke to John.

'Your intervention helped bring the real issues to the surface. Thanks.'

'You're welcome. And you were right to hold up the mirror and remind us all of our commitments.'

Dealing with Setbacks

Although the pilot implementation got off to a good start, it was inevitable that day-to-day business problems would swamp it at some point. Paradoxically, the risk is greater if the pilot is going well, because managers will assume it can take care of itself while they deal with more pressing matters.

When Philip sees the telltale signs that things aren't right, he views them as symptoms of a deeper problem: people haven't yet realised that some activities are not negotiable. Although it's only to be expected that managers like Dave will be drawn away from the pilot to deal with crises, it is the way the team respond to these setbacks that will determine whether they manage to attain the future state they are aiming for. This is why Philip is so adamant that John should hold a meeting with the whole management team to confront the issue.

At the meeting, people are reluctant to talk about the problems they face in front of the team – a common story where individuals are used to working independently or where there is insufficient trust to broach awkward topics. The problem is overcome when John puts the topic on the table, although he has to prompt people to ask for help.

Sometimes the causes of setbacks run much deeper, perhaps reflecting a lack of trust in the leader or a misalignment between individual objectives and company goals. In such cases, outside facilitation may be needed to bring issues out and help the group address them.

Supported by the renewed commitment of the plant management team, the pilot team spent the next two months putting in place the building blocks of the future-state operating system. On the assembly line, Steve and Fiona rebalanced the workload to *Takt* time. The improved process now needed three rather than four people. With John's approval, the fourth operator, Eileen, was retained until the end of the pilot to give the team additional capacity to refine and document the improvements in the assembly line. She was expected to take on a team leader role on another line at a later date.

Using a skills matrix to identify the gaps, Eileen worked with Fiona to develop on-the-job training for the assembly team. Fiona also worked with Louise and Philip on redrafting the team leader's roles and responsibilities to bolster the aspects of performance management, problem solving and process improvement that the pilot had shown to be weak.

In the mould shop, the data from the log sheets helped to pinpoint where losses were coming from. Derek set up a history book for each machine, which recorded standard settings for each part as well as any breakdowns that occurred and preventive maintenance that was done. Some machines suffered from minor stops that could easily be prevented; others had more complex problems that would only be resolved by the plant's electrical engineers.

Three months into the pilot implementation, changeovers were consistently below 40 minutes on the three mould machines dedicated to coffee makers, and it was time to switch to a pull system to control production. By way of preparation, the additional capacity released through improvements had been given over to building a safety stock of parts. This would ensure that deliveries weren't jeopardised during the transition – a vital precaution in light of the recent problems with Homestar.

Meanwhile, with Philip's help, Christine had worked with Dave and Trevor to establish the levels of 'shop stock' that would be needed at the two points where the flow would be broken, just before and after the assembly line. Once they had simulated the proposal on a spreadsheet to see how much stock was needed, the team held a meeting with Bill to agree how the pull system would work.

'In an ideal world, we'd keep the shop stock immediately after the mould machines, but that would involve changing the entire layout, so we'll put it in the warehouse to start with. Christine and Lisa have marked out the area.'

Philip explained that at the start of each day, the customer demand for coffee makers (which would initially be set at a fifth of the weekly demand) would be loaded into a levelling board in the warehouse using *kanban* cards.

'The levelling board is like a set of pigeonholes. Each column represents an hour, and each row represents a product variant. Every hour, Gaz Morgan in the warehouse will take the *kanbans* for the next hour and load those products into the despatch area for the next delivery.'

'What, even if there's no delivery due?' asked Bill.

'Yes. The levelling board sets the rhythm and pull for the entire plant, so it's important we do this every hour. In the long run, it'll help us develop the discipline to be much more flexible.'

'Sounds crackers!' Bill muttered. Philip heard him and was sure that others had. His behaviour was getting beyond a joke.

'Each pallet will have another *kanban* on it, which Mark will have put there when he packs the pallet on the assembly line. When Gaz moves the pallet, he needs to take this *kanban* out and put it into a collection box so that it can go back to the assembly line, where it will act as a signal to make more of that particular product.'

'Like a kind of loop,' said Fiona.

'Exactly. That's a good way of putting it. The pull system is basically a series of loops that connect the different stages of the value stream. It starts at the point nearest the customer and extends all the way back to the mould shop, and ultimately to our suppliers too.'

'So what happens when the *kanban* comes back to us at the assembly line? Do we change over immediately?'

'Ideally, yes, but not in the beginning. It would just cause chaos, because we aren't that good at changing over yet. To start with, we'll gather the *kanbans* together until we have, say, four boxes of the same variant – half a shift's worth – and then change over. As we get better, we can reduce this number and also reduce the stock of finished products.'

'But what about our economies of scale?' asked Bill. 'We've always processed large batches because it's cheaper that way. We took account of the cost of changing over when we optimised the batch sizes.'

'That's right,' said Philip. 'But that calculation probably doesn't take account of the cost of holding and managing stock, the risk of obsolescence, the extra lead time and so on. And when we reduce the changeover time, as we did in the mould shop, the cost will come down too.'

Bill was silent.

The group then walked through the process Philip had described, agreeing where the levelling board and collection points would go. Philip stressed the importance of establishing the new discipline in the first few weeks.

'There are bound to be a few teething problems; there always are. Someone will forget to remove the *kanbans* from the pallet and they'll get sent off to the customer by mistake or something. But the danger is that if we're not on top of these things, people will say the pull system doesn't work before it's even had a chance. It's up to us to enforce the discipline and make sure people wait for the *kanban*. When they see stocks getting low, they'll be tempted to change over before it arrives. We have to make sure they keep their nerve and wait for the signal.'

After the meeting had broken up Philip, half in a rage, went straight to John's office. He described angrily how Bill had run down the new way of working in front of everyone. 'John, believe me, we've tried to involve him at every turn, but it's had absolutely no effect.'

'I know. I've noticed it too,' John said, looking dejected. 'I think it's just too much for him after years of doing things the old way.'

'You're going to speak to him, aren't you?'

'I will.' John looked him in the eye. 'I promise.'

As he drove home, John ran through various ways of raising the topic with Bill in his mind, dismissing each one in turn. Whatever was he going to do?

Implementing a Pull System

Having established a platform of stability and the necessary level of flex-ibility, the team is now ready to bring everything together in a pull system. But while Philip sees this as the final phase in building something new, Bill sees it as the conclusive dismantling of a proven working method he's followed all his life. It's hardly surprising that the two men take such diver-gent views because the two methods of controlling production, push and pull, are diametrically opposed.

At its simplest, a pull system is a means of synchronising operations with true customer demand so that only the material required to meet that demand is released to the next stage in the process. By breaking down weekly orders into hourly demand for each product variant, the Arboria team have reduced the 'lumpiness' of customer demand. Instead of making a big batch of each product every week or two, production will now make each product every few days, and perhaps every day ultimately. Although this hourly demand is in a sense artificial, it sets the rhythm for the whole value stream and provides a mechanism whereby the operating system can be adapted as customer requirements change.

In principle, pull works like an invisible thread running through the process. When a customer buys an Arboria coffee maker, the thread tight-ens and pulls a single product through the value chain to replace it. In prac-tice, though, products still have to be produced in batches because the flexibility of the process is limited.

A push system can never emulate the flexibility and responsiveness of pull, since it depends on a set of assumptions about the process (such as defect rates and stock levels) that can't always hold true because of varia-tions in customer demand and the process itself over time. The only way to keep a traditional centrally driven system from collapsing is to reconcile the data manually and as often as possible, which ties up valuable resources in stocktaking and other activities. The advantage of pull is that feedback loops are built into the actual production system, allowing it to react to what is happening.

Another key difference is that a pull system entrusts the front line with much more responsibility. If Gaz forgets to remove the *kanban* from the pallet and return it to the upstream process, the parts that would have been ordered by that *kanban* won't get made. Because seemingly small actions or omissions can have enormous consequences, the new operating system has to be underpinned by new mindsets and behaviours.

The sustainability of a pull system depends as much on people's under-standing of why it is needed and what role they have to play as on the calculation of batch sizes, stock levels or signal points. In the pilot, those who have to change their way of working to ensure that pull works, such as Guy and Fiona, are more likely to develop such an understanding than those who haven't yet been through this experience.

As the sixteenth and final week of the pilot approached, Philip wondered how the team could make best use of Bruno's last visit. They had a great story to tell. They had achieved all their main objectives; indeed, exceeded them in the case of labour productivity. Most of the people involved had abandoned their initial scepticism about the new way of working, and some had become keen supporters.

Not everything was sweetness and light, though. A few cynics still maintained that things would go back to normal as soon as the bandwagon rolled out of town. Dave had told Philip about past initiatives that had withered as soon as senior managers' attention moved on. Reading between the lines, Philip wondered if the reason might have been Arboria's failure to recognise the contribution of front-line teams and middle managers. He knew from experience how crucial this was to successful change.

Philip is painfully aware that Arboria could lapse back into its former state. All too often, the performance line on the graph acts like elastic; it can be pulled up by a special effort, but soon springs back. It's one thing to create an island of excellence; another to transform a whole organisation and keep it that way.

Habits are hard to break; people revert to type. Bad memories of past improvement efforts can predispose an organisation to resist change. Conversely, a successful transformation can boost its ability to respond to challenges in future.

To transform Arboria's operations will call for a change in the organisation's culture.

CHAPTER 10

Embedding the Change

- A 'copy and paste' approach to scaling up the pilot won't work.
- There are four conditions for lasting behavioural change that need to be cultivated by managers.
- Developing a culture of continuous improvement depends on managing the impact of productivity improvements.

Many businesses are capable of running a successful pilot. The real challenge comes when they try to extend this success to the rest of their operations. Though Arboria has made a good job of implementing the pilot in its UK plant, its journey has only just begun. The hardest part still lies ahead: embedding change so that lean becomes a way of life, not just another initiative.

The language people use betrays how they think. People talk about 'rolling out' a change programme as though once the pilot has been completed, the real work is over, and all that remains is to replicate a winning formula elsewhere. If only that were true, change would be easy to manage.

In reality, though, a lean transformation involves changes that are too fundamental and deep-seated to be transferred elsewhere by a 'copy and paste' approach. Because operational excellence requires that operating system, management infrastructure and mindsets and behaviours are all changed at the same time, and because no two groups of people respond in the same way, each department, plant and office faces its own particular set of challenges.

The good news is that it's usually possible to transfer structural and technical (or process) changes relatively easily from one location to another, through documentation, training or other means. Changing mindsets and behaviours is another matter, and usually means people must experience for themselves what is required. Ensuring that people both understand the need for new ways of working and are truly committed to making them happen is central to embedding change in the organisation.

Integral to this process is the building of trust between the organisation and its leaders. Distrust between managers and workforce is a feature of most organisations and Arboria is no exception. People's attitudes are shaped by their personal experience of the discrepancy between promises and reality. If lean is to go beyond being a mere project to become a way of life, such ingrained distrust has to be dispelled – which is as big a challenge as it sounds.

Bruno's goals in undertaking a lean transformation are to make and sustain a step-change in Arboria's performance and establish the capabilities for continuous improvement. Although Dave understands the rationale for this strategy, he also sees the practical consequences: he and his colleagues will end up working harder and harder to keep improving performance until they work themselves out of a job. Such perceptions arise whenever managers try to convince their workforce to support a productivity improvement.

Once improvements have been achieved, managers face a dilemma. Should they lay people off at the risk of undermining support for the change process, or try to grow the business to absorb the improvements at the expense of delaying potential gains? Toyota offers some useful lessons in this respect. It treats its people not like commodities to be hired and fired as demand dictates, but as an integral and distinctive part of its business strategy. It believes that its core workforce gives it a competitive edge, and has designed its operating system accordingly. Such an ethos is a far cry from the governing principle of mass production: to free capital investment from dependence on labour. As the history of industrial relations attests, this hasn't been an easy path to follow.

Toyota's business system places great weight on investing in people, raising their skills and entrusting them with responsibility. Laying employees off would be the last resort. But most companies setting off on the lean journey haven't got this far. They have to cut costs, and lean seems to be a good way to do so. As their improvement efforts free up labour, they often cut their workforce without making any explicit commitment about the future.

So Bruno faces a tough challenge in embedding lean as a way of life. In shifting Arboria from its old business model to the new, he must decide what to do with the people who have been freed up by productivity gains: offer them voluntary redundancy, encourage early retirement or absorb them in growth areas within the business. Only then can he build a partnership between Arboria's management and workforce based on trust and aligned interests.

To celebrate the success of the pilot, John booked a suite at a greyhound track on the evening of Bruno and Dietmar's fourth and final visit to the plant. After long discussions about who should be invited, they agreed this should be a reward for the people who'd done the real work: the moulding and assembly teams, the lean team and the plant management team. Inevitably, there had been jokes made about Arboria going to the dogs.

Most of the party hadn't been greyhound racing before, and they had a wonderful time. The highlight came when the dog Bruno had backed won the sweepstake in the last race. Shouting over cries of, 'It's a fix!' Bruno offered to buy everyone a drink. Then he climbed onto a chair in the bar and made an emotional speech.

'You won't believe me, but I don't know how I picked the winner; in fact, I don't understand dog racing at all. Why do they chase this electric hare anyway? To be serious, though, winning the race is for me a kind of picture of what we have achieved with lean. I feel that we – or rather you – have come a long way, and I am very proud indeed. But this is just the beginning.'

'Here we go,' John whispered to Dave.

'Like my dog we have won one race, but now we want to train the whole organisation to be champions. It's up to you to do that here in Bolton, and up to me and Dietmar and the rest of ExCo to work out how we take this success to the other plants. You can be sure I'll be working on this as a priority now, and also that I'll continue to support you. But remember, this is just the start.'

At the next ExCo meeting a few weeks later, Dietmar summed up the main lessons from the pilot (see Figure 10.1).

Key success factors from the pilot

✓ Leadership from line managers, including active
involvement in ExCo

✓ Lean expertise (not just tools and techniques but also
experience of implementation)

✓ Full-time support team during implementation

✓ Thorough planning and effective progress reviews

✓ Quick wins to motivate production teams

✓ Willingness to challenge sacred cows (e.g. production planning)

arboria®

Figure 10.1 Key success factors from the pilot

'The pilot has shown us the importance of having the right people in the right roles. We had a full-time lean team to push the effort forward and support the line managers in the change process. We have seen that lean demands serious commitment from line managers, who need to lead by example. Senior managers must show the same kind of commitment too. I'd like to think that Bruno and I contributed to the pilot's success by visiting Bolton once a month, not just because of what we did while we were there but because we learned such a lot. And Philip's leadership of the lean team was crucial. We couldn't have done it without his experience and knowledge.'

'Isn't that a problem?' asked Arnaud Lefèvre, the sales and marketing director. 'Do we have a Philip in the other plants too?'

'It's a good question,' said Bruno. 'And one I've thought about a lot. It's true we don't have anyone else like Philip. So we have to decide whether to find someone for each plant, which means recruiting new people, or put Philip in a more European role to leverage his experience.'

'Isn't there a third option?' asked Jenny Plant, the finance director. 'Why can't we just get Philip to document what they've done and train some of our best people in the other plants on the processes to follow?'

'From what we saw of the pilot, I don't think that would work,' Dietmar replied.

'Well, that's how we introduced new accounting practices into the plants after the takeover. We got copies of the manuals and someone from the United States came over and trained all the management accountants. It worked well.'

'The trouble is, lean isn't as cut and dried as an accounting process,' Dietmar replied. 'The pilot showed us there are some changes that people don't find intuitive, and that challenge the way they've always worked. I don't think we can approach lean in the same way.'

'But if we recruit new people for each plant, we'll be going back to square one, and we just can't afford the time. Apart from the time it would take, think about the resources. We've got to remember this is an investment, and it has to pay back.'

Bruno stepped in. 'You have a point, Jenny, and six months ago I probably would have agreed with you. But what I've learned from the pilot is that lean is more than a series of process changes. It asks us to transform the way we work. If we get it right, it can be amazingly powerful, but it's also terribly fragile. If we break it, we won't get a second chance. We have to be prepared to over-invest if we need to.'

'But doesn't that mean all we are doing is pilots, over and over again?' Jenny persisted.

'No, I'm sure it doesn't. I'm sure there's some middle ground between the kind of roll-out you did for accounts and the pilot implementation we've just completed, but I'm not sure yet what it looks like.' Bruno paused. 'If I think about what has made the biggest impact on me over the past few months, it is the actual experience of implementing lean. It started when we visited the ATC plant; do you remember?'

People nodded.

'I didn't know what to expect, but I noticed that they did things in a completely different way. I remember talking to some of the people on the shop floor; do you remember Jerome? He knew exactly what he was doing and could explain how everything fitted together. Not even our plant managers could do that, and this guy was just a team leader. I admit I was scared to think the competition was so far ahead, but I was excited too. Now one of our plants has made the same journey. There is no substitute for experience, and so we need to find ways to repeat these experiences.'

Exploding the Myth of 'Pilot and Roll Out'

In alluding to ExCo's visit to ATC, Bruno articulates what it meant to him personally. Perhaps because she wasn't able to join the rest of the team on the visit, Jenny sees things much more straightforwardly. She believes all that's needed is for managers to define what needs to be done, provide the appropriate training and ensure the plan is implemented correctly.

Dietmar points out a fundamental distinction between Jenny's experience of the accounting changes and what needs to happen in a lean implementation.

Lean challenges people's basic beliefs about work. Deploying lean across an organisation entails repeating a cycle: raising people's awareness of a problem, engaging them in designing a better way of working, demonstrating its benefits, and finally creating the conditions for embedding the changes. In a sense, the task for executives is not to manage a single programme but to orchestrate a series of mini-transformations.

This can only work if people are engaged in the process. Those who will bear the consequences of change must have ownership of the outcome and take part in meaningful work to bring that change about. Change that is a joint effort rather than an imposition from on high stands a better chance of gaining cooperation and generating enthusiasm. Once it is 'our' programme rather than 'yours', new resources of ingenuity and previously untapped skills can be harnessed as people seize the opportunity to improve the quality of their working lives and get rid of long-standing frustrations.

Leading From the Top

It is essential that the senior team – ExCo in Arboria's case – take the lead in the deployment phase. Leadership shouldn't be delegated to a project team or an external consultant, for two reasons. First, people faced with change will take their cue from the boss when they gauge what their own commitment should be. What the boss says or doesn't say – and, more important, does or doesn't do – will influence how the rest of the organisation responds.

When a COO at a national bank e-mailed every employee to announce a new initiative to improve branch operations, but then devoted more time to overseeing the implementation of a new IT system, branch staff drew their own conclusions about the relative priorities of the two efforts.

The second reason for leading from the top is that only the senior team are in a position to address systems-level issues in the early stages. If, like Bruno and Dietmar, they have experienced these problems for themselves, they will have the necessary understanding and motivation to ensure the problems are properly addressed in the design of the lean programme. More important, they alone have the authority to take decisions to put things right.

The Line Manager's Role

As with the pilot, change must be implemented by line managers, not project teams. It is they who know best the people and equipment they are working with, and they who wield influence on the shop floor. Line managers are also well used to implementing decisions that have been made elsewhere in the organisation, something that will stand them in good stead when they work towards a new operating system that has already been partly defined during the pilot.

At Arboria, line managers like John and Dave already feel overloaded by the activities arising from the change programme. This is a common problem: those with the most valuable knowledge have the least time to share it. The best solution is to design a logical and efficient implementation process that captures lessons from the pilot so that line managers know what others have achieved and don't try to reinvent the wheel. For example, Philip could lead a small team in preparing training materials to explain what a pull system is and how it worked on the coffee machine line to help managers apply the system to other areas. In addition, providing opportunities for line managers from related areas to share their early experiences of lean helps to forge connections and build trust, and can provide a channel for spreading knowledge and new ideas.

One multinational oil company used a training game to launch each implementation wave. The game had small metal parts that simulated a maintenance intervention in which a major component has to be changed over for one of another size. Senior managers worked in teams with production and maintenance technicians to estimate how much they could reduce the time it took to assemble the parts without compromising safety. The game allowed people to see for themselves that huge improvements – far bigger than anyone predicted at the outset – could be made without heavy investment. Another lesson was that the elimination of unnecessary activities meant the improvements could have a beneficial effect on safety too. In the months that followed, participants cited the game as a catalyst in overturning the prevailing mindset that production performance could be improved only through capital expenditure.

In terms of management infrastructure, an obvious area for line managers to work on before and during implementation is the setting of new performance targets to reflect changes in the operating system. The pilot will have identified the key drivers of business performance, such as the OEE of the mould machines in Arboria's case. Using a generic value tree or cost model, managers in other areas can work out the operational targets they need to achieve to deliver business objectives.

This approach works best if managers carry out some of the data analysis themselves so they can gain a solid understanding of the principles and pitfalls involved. At Arboria, the manager of the German plant may be reluctant to accept that his site ought to be able to achieve a 30 to 40 per cent improvement just because the under-performing UK plant has done so. He is more likely to be persuaded if he gathers the data himself.

Engaging the Front Line

Managers need to consider how they will motivate their employees to support the lean effort. They might begin by asking shop floor teams to complete a survey anonymously, and follow up by discussing the findings. As well as revealing issues that need to be worked on, this can help initiate a dialogue about lean between management and workforce. The danger to avoid is that it becomes merely a box-ticking exercise that does not lead to concrete action.

As part of an operational improvement programme, one retail company asked its regional managers to assess the change readiness of the stores in their region. Drawing on data from an annual employee survey and their own in-depth knowledge, the managers segmented the stores as shown in Figure 10.2. This helped them decide which stores most needed support during implementation, and what form that support might take: limited coaching for a store that was already primed for change, or more extensive support for the regional manager whose region included stores that were reluctant to engage.

Being forced to think beyond the superficial process changes made the regional managers appreciate the importance of their own role in making change stick.

Managers are often preoccupied with rolling out an initiative as quickly as possible, since the rate of implementation is the key driver of improved financial return. Jenny argued for a faster deployment, and Bruno pointed out the risks. The implementation would fail to engage people if it were designed solely around processes (which can be changed quickly) rather than mindsets and working practices (which cannot). People take time to adapt to new expectations, especially where new ways of thinking and behaving are involved.

Skilled change leaders pull their teams along with them, taking care not to leave people behind. However frustrating this can be, it is counterproductive to push an organisation significantly faster than its people can go – something Bruno is learning in his lean journey. He has asked the UK plant to implement lean across the entire site within nine months; now he needs to ascertain whether he is being realistic.

After their evening at the dog track, John and Philip got together to work on a plan to meet Bruno's deadline. Although they knew it would be better to involve the entire management team, they feared that reaching agreement with a large group would involve weeks of delay.

The UK plant had five main product areas: coffee makers, kettles, toasters, blenders and others. 'Others' covered a variety of items with very low

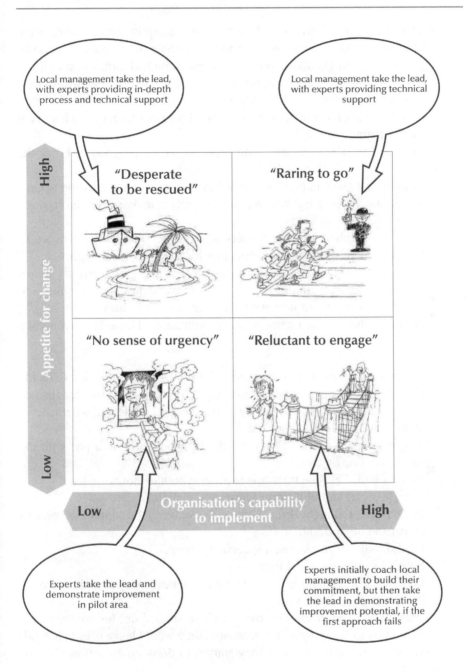

Figure 10.2 Assessing change readiness at the front line

order levels: some were new designs in the ramp-up phase, some were older products. There was a good chance that some of these would soon be dropped thanks to Dietmar's product review. John had a plan in mind.

'Why don't we get cracking on blenders? They're a nightmare, so they should give us the biggest bang for our buck.'

'OK, but we'll have to get our skates on if we hope to get anywhere near the target Bruno's set us.'

'We need to talk it through with Dave. It would be good to break the back of it before Christmas.'

Philip found Dave in the warehouse having a smoke and chatting to Gaz, who was loading up a truck with pallets of coffee makers. 'Hi. Everything OK?' he said to them both.

'Yep,' Gaz replied. 'Coffee makers is, anyway. This new system works like a dream. I wish I could say the same for the rest of it though.'

'Absolutely,' Dave added. 'The pull system is going fine, but it's shown what a state the rest of the business is in. We didn't have anything to compare it to before, but now we have, it looks a right mess.'

'Actually, that's what I came to talk to you about, Dave. Have you got a minute?'

'Sure.'

'I've just come from a meeting with John, and we've decided to tackle blenders next. We need to get a move on if we're to meet the deadline of implementing lean across the site by next June. So I wondered whether . . .'

'Next June!' Dave was shocked.

'Yes, didn't you know? Bruno wants the whole site on a par with the coffee maker line by then.'

'Bloody hell! Does he think *we're* all greyhounds now or what?'

'I know it's tight, but we don't have much choice.'

'Why's that? I thought Bruno said he'd give us all the support we needed in the bar the other night.'

'He did, but . . . you know, a speech is a speech.'

'So it's business as usual then.'

'Look, I know it's not ideal, but we've got to find a way to make it work.'

'If there is one,' Dave said.

Later that day, after mulling over it, Dave spelled out his concerns. He feared that by rushing the implementation, they would leave people behind. Philip heard him out, and then they started to draw up an action plan for implementation.

The following week Philip, Lisa and Steve held a session with the team leaders responsible for blenders. Dave had been called away to sort out a problem with raw materials, and got back just as the meeting ended.

'How did it go?' he asked.

'OK, I think.' Philip sounded doubtful. 'They didn't say much, but they seemed happy enough.'

Philip and the team set to work to prepare for the kick-off meeting for blender staff to be held the following Monday.

When Monday came, however, the blender team were hard pressed to meet the day's deliveries, so the meeting was cut to a half-hour session in the canteen during the shift handover. After running through his presentation, Philip asked for questions. There weren't any. He knew this was a bad sign, but it was time to get back to the shop floor, so he brought the meeting to a close.

Dave came over. 'OK?' he asked.

'I don't know,' said Philip, uneasily. 'What do you think?'

'They're very quiet. It's not like them at all. We'll know this time tomorrow what they think.'

Dave was right; they did know the next day. It was like a bomb going off, and it was the performance monitoring board that had lit the fuse. Steve was discussing it with Malcolm Jones, the team leader on the blender assembly line. The discussion got heated, several more people joined in, and one operator complained he was sick of being treated like a barrel-organ monkey who was expected always to dance to the management's tune.

When Philip arrived, the team gathered around him, all shouting at once. He didn't often feel out of his depth, but he did now. Noticing something was wrong, Dave ambled over from the coffee maker line.

'Is there a problem?' he asked mildly, and was almost deafened. 'Hang on, hang on! If everyone shouts at once nobody will get heard. Why don't the rest of you get back to work while I have a quiet word with Malcolm and Philip. We'll come and see you shortly, but first I'm going to get to the bottom of this. OK?'

As the operators drifted back to work, Dave asked Malcolm what had gone wrong.

Malcolm threw up his hands. 'I don't understand this place. Why do they always spring things on us? First the new targets, then yesterday's meeting, and then this new board, all out of the blue, no consultation, no warning, nothing.'

'What do you think we should do?' Philip asked.

Dave took a while to reply. 'There's nothing to do but let everybody calm down a bit. Then we'd better find out what they have to say. We'll tell them that provided we get the day's quota made by seven o'clock, we'll set aside an hour in the training room to clear the air.'

Malcolm nodded.

'OK by me,' Philip agreed.

Malcolm went back to the line and spoke to everyone in turn. Eventually, he returned to say that the team agreed to the meeting. Dave proposed the three of them get together with Steve to discuss how to handle it.

In the meeting room, Dave took the initiative once again.

'What do we want to achieve in the blender line? Let's see if we can make a list. For example, make the equipment more reliable', he explained, writing on a flipchart.

'Right tools for the job,' Malcolm added with feeling.

'Quicker changeovers?' offered Philip.

Dave hesitated, his pen hovering over the chart. 'That's what *we* want; how do we translate that into the operators' language?'

'Smaller batches?' Steve suggested.

'Smaller batches mean more changeovers,' Malcolm said. 'I thought we were trying to calm things down!'

'How about fewer unnecessary changeovers and better planning?' Dave suggested.

'Spot on,' Malcolm agreed.

They continued until they had filled the page.

'Here's my suggestion,' Dave said. 'We turn this page over and then ask the team the same question we've just answered when they come in at seven o' clock.'

'You mean ask them to set out the objectives of the lean transformation?' Philip was dubious.

'More or less, but phrase it differently to pick up on their frustrations. Maybe something like: what are the problems you want resolved?'

'You mean resolved by lean?' Steve asked.

'I do mean that, but I don't think we need use the word. If we're not confident that lean will address their problems, we're doing the wrong thing, aren't we?' Nobody demurred. 'Depending on how the meeting goes, we can turn the page back over at the end and show them we're all after the same things.'

It took a moment for Dave's suggestion to sink in. Steve spoke first.

'Isn't there a risk that you'll come across as a bit of a smart arse? You know, like, "Here's the one we prepared earlier."'

'Not necessarily: it all depends on how it's done,' Malcolm said, looking at Dave. 'I think it will work as long as Dave does it.'

Seven o'clock came, and the team trooped into the training room. Dave ran the meeting along the lines he had proposed. He asked the team for their concerns and discussed each one in turn, writing it up as he went along.

When everyone had said his or her bit, Dave summed up. 'I understand the frustrations you've raised; in fact, I share most of them. An awful lot of problems need fixing if we're to improve this plant. The great thing is that we all agree on what they are. In case you don't believe me, I've got something to show you. Before the meeting, we jotted down what we want the lean programme to achieve. Here's our list.' Dave turned over the page. There was silence as people took it in. 'It should look pretty familiar.'

'It does,' said one of the women. 'But it's a pity nobody bothered to talk to us about it before.'

'You're right. We could have handled it a lot better,' said Dave. 'But let that be water under the bridge. I hope you'll remember this meeting in weeks to come because it shows how much we have in common. For our part, we'll undertake to listen to you more in future. What I ask of you is that you give the new approach your best shot. We all know we've got to improve to stay competitive, and none of us wants things to stay as they are now. I know I don't.'

'Thanks, Dave.' Philip stood up. 'Dave's said everything that needed to be said, but I just wanted to apologise to you all for poor communication earlier. Sometimes you can't see what needs to be done until it's too late. That's what happened to me today, anyway.'

It wasn't every day that the Arboria workforce heard a manager apologise. It was a new experience for Philip too.

After the blender team had left, Philip slapped Dave on the back. 'Thanks, Dave. Brilliant job. I learned a lot from you today. I can see now that you tried to warn me this might happen, but I didn't take it in. If it ever happens again, make sure I'm listening!'

'No problem', Dave said, embarrassed. 'They're good guys; they just need to be handled right. They'll come round. No damage done.'

Developing the Conditions for Lasting Change

In a bid to capture the benefits of lean as quickly as possible, Bruno has set a highly ambitious deadline for the UK management team. It would be a tall order to change the process and layout in nine months, let alone people's mindsets and behaviour. While Bruno and ExCo grapple with the task of transferring the approach to Arboria's other plants, John and Philip have already started to take shortcuts and are discovering the risks they present.

To achieve lasting behavioural change, managers need to ensure that four interrelated factors are in place: understanding and commitment, role modelling, capability building and aligned systems and structures (see Figure 10.3).

'I will change my behaviour if ...'

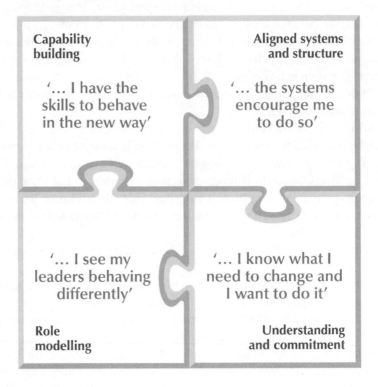

Figure 10.3 Conditions for lasting behavioural change

These factors can be used like a checklist. For example, if Philip had been thinking about understanding and commitment, he might have asked himself: can I imagine Malcolm saying 'I know what I need to change and I want to do it'? If he couldn't, he might have realised that he and others hadn't spent enough time with Malcolm to explain why Arboria was going lean and what the benefits would be for him, and he might have avoided antagonising the blender team.

Unlike Guy and Fiona and their teams in the pilot area, who had the opportunity to develop a personal understanding of the potential for improvement through the diagnostic process, the blender team were merely told what to do. When Dave was unable to attend the kick-off meeting, they could have interpreted his absence as lack of interest. They look to him, as a well-respected figure on the shop floor, to provide cues for their own behaviour. In turn, Malcolm acts as a role model for his team.

Building capabilities is a task that managers tend to understand better, although they may assume that a few classroom-based training sessions will do the trick. Arboria's pilot implementation raised doubts as to whether team leaders had the right skills to implement change and manage the new lean system. This is exactly the kind of systems-level issue that senior managers need to address to prevent the problems encountered in the pilot being repeated in each successive wave of implementation.

The fourth condition for lasting change is the alignment of systems and structures to provide the right incentives for behavioural change. An obvious example is the use of performance management to focus people's attention on the right things and link personal goals with business objectives. But the problem over the performance monitoring board on the blender line shows that even clear performance targets can be counterproductive if people don't understand why they are being introduced or how they will be used.

Dave managed to rescue a tricky situation by bridging the gap between what senior managers want to achieve and what front-line people understand and are capable of contributing to the change effort. Though aware of the gap, Philip hadn't realised how dangerous it could be.

Dave made a couple of important changes to the way the lean programme was communicated to the production team. First, he positioned lean as the answer to their problems, not the source of them, and let the operators speak for themselves instead of trying to second-guess their concerns. Second, he took care to use language that reflected the production team's point of view so as to make the communication meaningful.

Dave's experience on the coffee maker line led him to believe that because lean eliminates sources of loss, it should serve the interests of workforce as well as management. Waste is at least as frustrating to an operator who assembles blenders all day long as it is to Philip, John or Bruno. Dave also believed the production workers were best placed to identify problems because they encountered them every day.

Philip believed Dave had saved the day. But whether his intervention would be enough to put the team back on track after a dangerous detour remained to be seen.

The next day, Philip told John what had happened.

'I can't say it surprises me,' John said. 'That blender team are a cynical bunch.'

'Maybe, but they have some justification.'

'How come?'

'Their biggest concern yesterday – and that's not just the team, but Malcolm and Dave too – was that we aren't listening to them. Let's be honest, John, we know we're rushing all this. Yesterday showed me that we've been cutting corners. Or I have, at any rate.'

'Such as?'

'We reduced the kick-off meeting to half an hour . . .'

'Only because we were behind on production.'

'Hang on, John, let me finish. We reduced the kick-off to half an hour, which meant we had to skip questions and discussion. We didn't involve Malcolm beforehand. We decided not to involve the whole management team in planning implementation to save time. We chose to take on the hardest area of the plant at the most difficult time of year. We . . .'

'OK, Phil, I get the message.'

'I haven't finished yet. I realised yesterday that Dave had been trying to warn me we were heading for trouble, but I hadn't been listening. Yesterday's experience, which I wouldn't want to repeat in a hurry, taught me that Dave is like our AWACS plane.'

'Our what?'

'AWACS – those planes with radar equipment that fly around checking for trouble. Dave's been picking up bad vibes and sending us signals, but we've been so engrossed in our plans that we've ignored him.'

'That's putting it a bit strong, Phil. Still, I see what you mean, though I can't say I've ever thought of Dave that way myself.' John tilted back in his chair, which creaked in protest, and gazed up at the ceiling.

Resisting the urge to make a suggestion, Philip let John consider what he'd said.

'I've been thinking back to the pilot,' John said at length, 'and it's true that we, and Bruno for that matter, have gone from being closely involved to managing at a distance. From the operators' point of view, it must feel like the party's over and now life's back to normal. So perhaps we should slow down a bit. Any thoughts?'

'Maybe we need to take the time to do a mini version of the diagnostic we did in coffee makers. That worked well as a way of uncovering the issues and engaging people in what we were trying to do. Of course, if we do this then we'll have to rethink the nine-month timescale.'

John agreed. 'But if we go back to Bruno without some sort of proposal, he'll have us for breakfast. Can you draft a memo, and then we'll talk it through?'

'No problem.'

Over the next couple of days, Philip worked with Dave and a few others to put together a plan showing the timing and sequence of the lean implementation for the whole plant, area by area. This exercise showed that if their assumptions were correct, the implementation would take between 18 months and two years to complete. They all felt this was more realistic than their original target of nine months. They also thought most of the estimated bottom-line improvement could be captured in the first year, given that blenders, an area of high potential, was first in line.

While Philip busied himself with the proposal, John had business of his own, and it was something he'd been putting off for a long time. He arranged to go for a pub lunch with Bill. On the way, he broached the subject that had been bothering him for months.

'Bill, there's something we need to talk about.'

'I know,' Bill replied.

'You do? Good. It's just that . . . well, I think we both know this lean thing is a big change, and . . .'

Bill helped him out. 'It's not just a big change, John; it's a whole new way of working. And it doesn't suit me at all.'

'Oh?' John was taken aback. 'So you've thought about this?'

'Of course I have! For a while I couldn't think about anything else. To begin with, I was pretty angry, what with Philip coming in with his clever ideas and all. But – and this may sound strange – I can see now that it might work.'

John could hardly believe this was Bill speaking.

'Not only that, I can see the business needs to go down this route if it's going to survive and grow.'

'You amaze me!'

'So I've decided it's time to move on. This is the right road for Arboria, but it isn't the right road for me.'

They arrived at the pub and went in. While Bill found a table, John went to the bar and ordered two pints of bitter. He couldn't help seeing the funny side. It had taken him all this time to speak to Bill, and now they had sorted everything out on the way to the pub. He paid for the drinks and sat down.

'Cheers!'

'Cheers,' Bill echoed.

'There's something I'm curious about,' John said.

'Yes?'

'What makes you so sure that lean is right for Arboria, but not for you?'

'Well, it's like this,' said Bill. 'I realised I wasn't needed any more.'

'But you could always find another role.'

'I know, but I don't need another role, and I don't want one either. Look, John, I'm a planning manager, I've been one all my life, and if a business this complicated can run without one, it's got to be better that way. So it's time for me to step aside. You can't teach an old dog new tricks – not this one, anyhow.'

Bill smiled as if to reassure his friend that he was happy to go. 'Now I've got a question for you.'

'Fire away.'

'If the business can run without a planning manager, what does the future hold for the general manager?'

Developing a Continuous Improvement Culture

The ability to achieve continuous improvement is the ultimate goal of the lean journey. Though the three dimensions of the change platform still need to be tackled in an integrated way, their relative importance alters at this stage. To be sure, the operating system must be adapted to meet changing customer requirements and accommodate new products and technologies, but developing a culture of continuous improvement is likely to depend more on a robust management infrastructure and the right mindsets and behaviour. The ability to improve performance year after year has less to do with lean tools and techniques than with a comprehensive, robust cycle of setting and tracking improvement goals led by the organisation's senior executives.

The site-wide implementation plan put together by Philip and Dave as the basis for the discussion with Bruno typifies the kind of activity that now needs to be integrated into the budgetary and planning cycle at Arboria. The detailed planning and clear target setting that contributed to the success of the pilot must become the norm rather than the exception. Regular reviews tailored to the different levels of the organisation will be needed to manage performance, and mechanisms must be put in place to highlight issues requiring action from more senior managers.

Such processes can have considerable impact. At one specialist chemicals producer two years into its lean journey, managers cited the introduction of an effective performance stewardship process as the single most important factor in winning capital productivity gains of over 10 per cent.

Arboria will need to bolster its capabilities by establishing a dedicated pool of trained people to support line managers as they implement lean in their areas of responsibility. Once operations become more stable, these line managers will also need coaching and support as they find that the fire-fighting skills that served them well in the past are no longer at a premium. Instead, they will need to develop new skills to identify and eliminate the sources of loss in their value streams, as well as the leadership skills to help instil the new behaviours that lean requires.

All in all, developing a continuous improvement culture will challenge the roles and perceptions of everyone in the organisation. Bill is right to question the future role of the general manager. The journey to lean will change every job at Arboria.

As we've seen, lean isn't a project, an initiative, a programme or a cost-cutting approach. It's a whole new way of doing business that depends on aligning a whole organisation around a clear and attractive vision of how it will function in future. Lean starts from the customer's perspective and does whatever it takes to flow value to the customer as efficiently as possible and at the lowest cost. It asks front-line employees to work in more productive ways and to trust their managers and leaders, who must rise to the challenge of growing the business to absorb productivity gains. Similarly, it asks leaders to entrust front-line employees with real responsibility and autonomy.

As a journey, lean isn't a walk in the park or a hike in the woods; it's a full-scale expedition.

When the Arboria team started out on their lean journey, they had little idea what to expect. Month by month, they derived benefits from their experience: productivity improvements, new ways of working, fresh thinking. At each stage, the new vantage point gave them a better appreciation of what lay ahead, encouraging them to persevere despite the difficulties. They rose to the challenge of the journey and at the same time developed as a team, spurred on by the objective they were pursuing. Excellence is inspiring: it's the destination that we never quite reach, but that draws us ever onwards on the journey.

Characters work for Arboria and are based at its Bolton plant unless otherwise indicated.

Arnaud Lefèvre, international sales and marketing director (Brussels)

Bill Moran, planning manager

Brian Johnson, finance manager

Bruno Fontana, chief executive officer (Brussels)

Christine McGuire, production planner

Dave Smith ("Donkey Dave"), production manager

Derek Hines, senior maintenance engineer

Dietmar Schaeffer, demand fulfilment director (Brussels)

Eileen Mayoh, operator, coffee maker assembly line

Fiona Richardson, team leader, coffee maker assembly line

Gaz Morgan, warehouse operator

Guy Lanbridge, shift supervisor, mould shop

Howard Ashworth, operator, coffee maker assembly line

Jeff Aspinall, operator, coffee maker assembly line

Jenny Plant, finance director (Brussels)

Jerome Chevalier, team leader, ATC, Rouen

John Wexford, general manager, UK plant

Lisa Hallum, production engineer

Louise Bradley, personnel manager

Luc Bezier, production manager, ATC, Rouen

Malcolm Jones, team leader, blender assembly line

Mark Sherwell, operator, coffee maker assembly line

Philip Hargreaves, lean implementation manager

Philippe de Lasset, managing director, Maison de Lasset, Orléans (Arboria distributor)

Steve Edwards, production engineer

Trevor Radcliffe, maintenance manager

By now you will have spent a long time thinking about the journey to lean, what it involves, and the obstacles and pitfalls you might encounter along the way. We have drawn on our own experiences to portray the journey as realistically as we could. Though the benefits that companies can reap from successful lean implementation are huge, the journey remains a perilous one. A lot of companies fall by the wayside, or don't manage to fulfil the high expectations they had when they set out.

It takes a lot of courage and energy to keep a company moving forward until it reaches its goal. Not just management but the entire organisation must be fully committed, even though the path and the destination are unlikely to be clear at the outset. Though the going can be tough, many companies we know have overcome the difficulties and achieved successful lean transformations.

We leave you with one last question: what is your motivation in embarking on the journey to lean? There are two main reasons why companies undertake lean transformations: to adopt a better system of production or to achieve a change in culture.

Companies in the first category see lean as an opportunity to take their operations to a higher plane, the top of a new S-curve. By adopting and adapting the operating methods used by some of the world's leading companies, they seek to open up new business opportunities and deliver their products or services in a fraction of the usual lead times. The potential competitive advantage this offers prompts many organisations to embark on the lean journey.

Companies in the second category regard lean as a way of galvanising their organisation around a common goal and way of working. Lean represents for them a new source of inspiration and energy, capable of motivating people and boosting performance to new levels. As Arboria's story demonstrates, it can act as a formidable means for CEOs to turn around their entire operations and bring about wholesale transformation even as it works on specific and concrete tasks.

We hope this book will help you with your own transformation and wish you good luck on your journey to lean.

Appendix Types of Loss, Symptoms, Possible Causes, Key Tools and Techniques

Type of loss	Symptoms	Possible causes	Key tools & techniques
Overproduction Producing sooner, faster or in greater quantities than is needed by the customer	Too many parts are produced Parts are produced too early Parts accumulate in uncontrolled inventories Long manufacturing lead times Poor delivery performance	Long changeovers driving large batch sizes Use of an economic algorithm to determine batch sizes Poor scheduling Confusion over schedule priorities Unbalanced material flow Prioritisation of equipment utilisation as a key metric	Just-in-Time (continuous flow processing, *Takt*, pull systems, levelled production) Changeover reduction or SMED (where changeovers are driving batch sizes)
Waiting Idle time (for people or machines) in which no value-adding activities take place	Operators often wait for materials or information Operators stand and watch machines run Operators often wait for unavailable machines Long in-process delays Low productivity Long manufacturing lead times	Large batch sizes upstream causing material shortages Poor supplier delivery performance or quality Poor machine condition (low OEE) Poor scheduling Poor labour utilisation Lack of flexibility in skills	Flexible labour systems (including standardised work) Just-in-Time (continuous flow processing, *Takt*, pull systems, levelled production) Strategic maintenance Supplier development

Appendix continued

Type of loss	Symptoms	Possible causes	Key tools & techniques
Transportation Unnecessary movement of materials	Multiple handling or movement of parts Excessive handling damage Long distances travelled by parts between processes Long manufacturing lead times High indirect costs due to storage space and material handling equipment required	Sequential processes physically separated Poor layout High inventories; same part often held in multiple locations	Continuous flow processing and pull systems Workplace organisation
Over-processing Effort that isn't required by the customer and adds no value	Performing of processes that aren't required by the customer Redundant approval requirements Higher direct costs than competitors	Over-engineered processes Product design Unclear customer specifications Excessive testing Inappropriate policies or procedures	Production preparation Standardised work

Type of loss	Symptoms	Possible causes	Key tools & techniques
Inventory Any parts or materials above the minimum required to deliver what customers want when they want it	Obsolete stock Cashflow problems Lack of space Long manufacturing lead times Poor delivery performance Extensive rework needed when quality problems are identified	Overproduction Poor forecasting or scheduling High levels of safety stock because of frequent process or quality problems Purchasing policies Unreliable suppliers Large batch sizes	Just-in-Time (continuous flow processing, *Takt*, pull systems, levelled production) Standardised work Supplier development Strategic maintenance (where process problems are driven by equipment issues) Statistical process control (where process problems are driven by quality issues)
Motion Unnecessary movement of people or materials within a process	Searching for tools or parts Excessive walking by operators Double handling of parts Low productivity	Poor layout of workplace, tools and materials Lack of visual controls Poor process design	Workplace organisation Continuous flow processing Motion *kaizen* Standardised work Visual management

Appendix continued

Type of loss	Symptoms	Possible causes	Key tools & techniques
Rework Repetition or correction of a process	Dedicated rework processes High defect rates High material costs because of spoilage levels Low productivity Large quality or inspection departments	Poor-quality materials Poor machine conditions Unstable or incapable[1] processes Low skill levels Unclear customer specifications	Statistical process control Autonomation Strategic maintenance Supplier development Standardised work
Variability Any deviation from the standard or nominal condition	High levels of scrap or rework Large quality or inspection departments Recurring problems that are patched up with quick fixes Output measures that show an unacceptable level of variation (e.g. quality)	Unstable or unpredictable processes Incapable processes Poor quality materials or supplied parts Low skill levels	Statistical process control Autonomation Supplier development Standardised work

Note: [1] Stable and predictable processes that can't deliver parts within specifications

Type of loss	Symptoms	Possible causes	Key tools & techniques
Inflexibility Response to demand variability Issues that arise as a result of variation in customer demand	Unable to react quickly to changes in customer demand High levels of overtime Periods of under-utilisation	High inventories Long changeover times Poorly balanced work Low skill levels Over-scoped equipment	Just-in-Time (continuous flow processing, *Takt*, pull systems, levelled production) Flexible labour systems Changeover reduction or SMED
Working practices Normal working practices that obstruct flexibility in the operating system	Unable to change ways of working significantly Work frequently delayed when the right people aren't available	Terms and conditions not configured to facilitate change Operators are highly specialised and often only one person can do a specific job	Standardised work Flexible labour systems

John Drew is an Expert in McKinsey & Company's Manufacturing Practice. He works with companies designing and implementing lean production systems and has particular experience in the change management aspects of lean implementation. John trained at McKinsey's Production System Design Centre before going on to work with organisations in various sectors including automotive, electronics, aerospace, chemicals, banking and retail. Prior to joining McKinsey John worked in the packaging industry for CarnaudMetalbox and in the supplier development function at Land Rover. He holds a Masters degree in Engineering, Economics and Management from Oxford University.

Blair McCallum is a Partner at McKinsey & Company where he founded the Production Systems Design Centre in the United Kingdom. He has helped companies in a variety of industries to transform their operations by applying lean principles in diverse sectors, including oil and gas, automotive, aerospace, furniture, defence and construction. Previously, at Toyota, he was responsible for building the company's base of European suppliers and converting them to the Toyota Production System. He then took charge of the Rover Group's supplier base and its five main plants, where he introduced lean principles into the manufacture of new products, such as the Rover 75.

Stefan Roggenhofer is a Partner at McKinsey & Company and a leader of its Manufacturing Practice in Europe. Based in France, he has led engagements in operational performance improvement in a diverse range of sectors, including for clients in luxury goods, aerospace, consumer electronics and steel. His special focus is behavioural change during transformation efforts. Before joining McKinsey, Stefan was responsible for marketing and sales of assembly systems at Prodel SA. He was previously an engineer in the field of aerodynamic studies at Aerospatial. He holds a Masters degree in Engineering from the Technical University of Munich and an MBA from INSEAD in France.

The authors have been assisted by David Birch, who took the lead role in developing the material in Chapter 4, and by Ivan Hutnik.

David Birch is a Partner at McKinsey & Company and a leader of its Manufacturing Practice in the United Kingdom, and is one of the firm's leading practitioners in the area of operational performance improvement, where he has served clients in many sectors, including aerospace, chemicals and transportation. At Mars Confectionery before joining McKinsey, David held a variety of management positions in production, technical services, product development and industrial engineering.

Ivan Hutnik is a specialist in communications and knowledge management in the context of organisational change. He is a psychotherapist with an interest in the effects of organisational design on human behaviour and has worked as a coach to senior executives in leadership effectiveness. He has served clients in a wide range of industries including automotive, consumer goods, financial services, pharmaceuticals, paper and steel.

Index